THE ULTIMATE BEER FERMENTATION HANDBOOK

From Ale to Lager to Stout – Learn Everything You Need to Know About DIY Beer Fermentation, Yeast Selection and Advanced Brewing Techniques.

SAMUEL H. GILBERT

All rights reserved. No part of this book may be reproduced, stored in a retrieval system, or transmitted in any form or by any means—electronic, mechanical, photocopying, recording, or otherwise—without the prior written permission of the publisher, except for brief quotations used in reviews.

Copyright © 2024 by Samuel H. Gilbert

CONTENTS

Introduction — 6
   The Art and Science of Beer Fermentation — 6
   History and Evolution of Beer Brewing — 6

CHAPTER 1 — 8

Understanding the Basics of Fermentation — 8
   1.1 What is Fermentation? — 8
   1.2 Types of Fermentation in Beer Production — 9
   1.3 Ingredients in Fermentation: Yeast, Malt, Water, and Hops — 11

CHAPTER 2 — 13

The Beer Brewing Process — 13
   2.1 Overview of the Brewing Process — 13
   2.2 The Malting Process: From Grain to Malt — 14
   2.3 Mashing and Lautering: Extracting Sugars — 15

CHAPTER 3 — 20

The Role of Yeast in Beer Fermentation — 20
   3.1 Types of Yeast Used in Brewing — 20
   3.2 Yeast Propagation and Maintenance — 21
   3.3 The Fermentation Process: Primary and Secondary Fermentation — 22

CHAPTER 4 — 27

Fermentation Equipment and Setup — 27
   4.1 Essential Equipment for Home Brewing — 27
   4.2 Setting Up a Fermentation Space — 30
   4.3 Sanitization and Cleanliness in Brewing — 32

CHAPTER 5 — 34

Controlling Fermentation Variables — 34
   5.1 Temperature Control During Fermentation — 34
   5.2 Monitoring and Adjusting pH Levels — 35

    5.3 Oxygen Management in Fermentation   37

CHAPTER 6   40
Beer Styles and Fermentation Profiles   40
6.1 Ales: Fermentation Characteristics and Styles   40
6.2 Lagers: Cold Fermentation and Maturation   42
6.3 Specialty Beers: Sours, Stouts, and Beyond   45

CHAPTER 7   49

Packaging and Carbonation   49
7.1 Bottling vs. Kegging: Pros and Cons   49
7.2 Carbonation Methods: Natural vs. Forced   52
7.3 Storing and Aging Beer   54

CHAPTER 8   59

Recipe Development and Experimentation   59
8.1 Designing Your Own Beer Recipes   59
8.2 Experimenting with Ingredients and Techniques   63
8.3 Scaling Recipes for Larger Batches   68

CHAPTER 9   74

The Science Behind Flavour and Aroma   74
9.1 Understanding Flavour Profiles in Beer   74
9.2 The Role of Hops in Aroma and Bitterness   78
9.3 How Fermentation Influences Flavour Complexity   81

CHAPTER 10   84

Advanced Fermentation Techniques   84
10.1 High Gravity Brewing and Fermentation   84
10.2 Barrel Aging and Secondary Fermentation   86
10.3 Using Wild Yeasts and Bacteria for Unique Flavors   88

CHAPTER 11   91

Troubleshooting Common Fermentation Issues   91
11.1 Identifying Off-Flavours and Their Causes   91

    11.2 Dealing with Stuck Fermentations   93
    11.3 Preventing and Addressing Contamination   95

Conclusion   98

appendix   99
    Glossary of Brewing and Fermentation Terms   99

PROJECTs   103
    1. Ale Brewing Process   103
    2. Lager Brewing Process   104
    3. Sour Brewing Process   105
    4. Stout Brewing Process   107

INTRODUCTION

The Art and Science of Beer Fermentation

Beer fermentation is a fascinating blend of art and science that has been practiced for thousands of years. At its core, fermentation is a natural process where yeast, a tiny but powerful microorganism, converts sugars into alcohol and carbon dioxide. This transformation is what gives beer its alcohol content and carbonation, as well as many of its flavours and aromas.

From a scientific perspective, fermentation is a controlled biochemical reaction. Brewers carefully select ingredients, manage conditions like temperature and pH, and monitor the progress to ensure that the yeast works its magic effectively. The type of yeast used, along with the ingredients and brewing techniques, plays a significant role in determining the style and taste of the final beer.

But fermentation is more than just a chemical process—it's also an art. Experienced brewers understand that small adjustments in timing, temperature, or ingredient ratios can lead to subtle but important differences in the flavour and character of the beer. This is where the art of brewing shines, as brewers use their knowledge, intuition, and creativity to craft beers with unique and desirable qualities.

In summary, beer fermentation is the perfect marriage of art and science. The scientific aspects ensure consistency and safety, while the artistic elements allow for creativity and innovation, making each beer a unique experience.

History and Evolution of Beer Brewing

Beer brewing is one of the oldest crafts known to humanity, with a rich history that dates back thousands of years. The origins of beer can be traced to ancient civilizations like the Sumerians and Egyptians, who discovered that grains could be fermented to create a flavourful and intoxicating beverage. Early beer was often brewed in homes and temples, and it quickly became a central part of daily life and religious rituals.

As time passed, beer brewing techniques spread across different cultures and regions, each adding their own twist to the process. In medieval Europe, monasteries became the hubs of brewing innovation. Monks refined brewing methods, developed new recipes, and even introduced hops as a key ingredient, which not only flavoured the beer but also acted as a natural preservative.

The Industrial Revolution in the 18th and 19th centuries brought significant advancements to beer brewing. New machinery allowed for large-scale production, making beer more accessible to the masses. This era also saw the rise of commercial breweries, which began to standardize recipes and improve the consistency and quality of beer.

In the 20th century, beer brewing continued to evolve with the introduction of refrigeration, pasteurization, and scientific advancements in microbiology. These innovations made it possible to produce a wider variety of beer styles and to brew with greater precision and control. The craft beer movement of the late 20th and early 21st centuries further revolutionized the industry, as small, independent breweries began experimenting with new flavours, ingredients, and techniques, bringing beer brewing back to its artisanal roots.

Today, beer brewing is a global phenomenon, with countless styles and traditions. From ancient brews to modern craft beers, the history and evolution of beer brewing is a testament to human creativity, ingenuity, and the enduring appeal of this beloved beverage.

CHAPTER 1

UNDERSTANDING THE BASICS OF FERMENTATION

1.1 What is Fermentation?

Fermentation is a natural process that has been used for centuries to create a variety of foods and beverages, including beer. At its simplest, fermentation is a biochemical reaction where microorganisms like yeast or bacteria convert sugars into alcohol, gases, and other by-products. This process is what gives beer its alcohol content, carbonation, and many of its complex flavours.

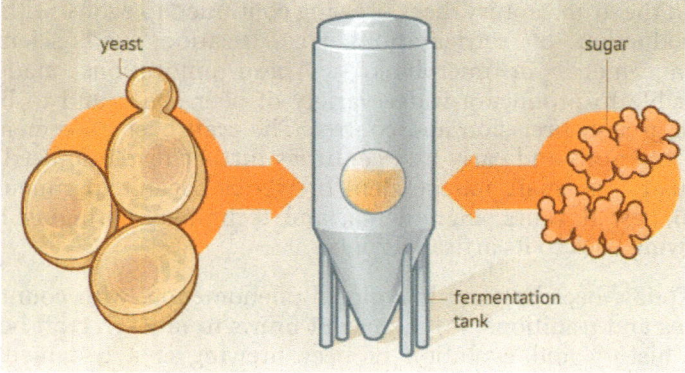

In the context of beer brewing, fermentation occurs when yeast is added to the wort (a sugary liquid made from malted grains). The yeast consumes the sugars in the wort and produces alcohol and carbon dioxide as waste products. The carbon dioxide creates the bubbles in beer, while the alcohol provides the intoxicating effect. Along the way, the yeast also produces a range of flavours and aromas that contribute to the beer's overall character.

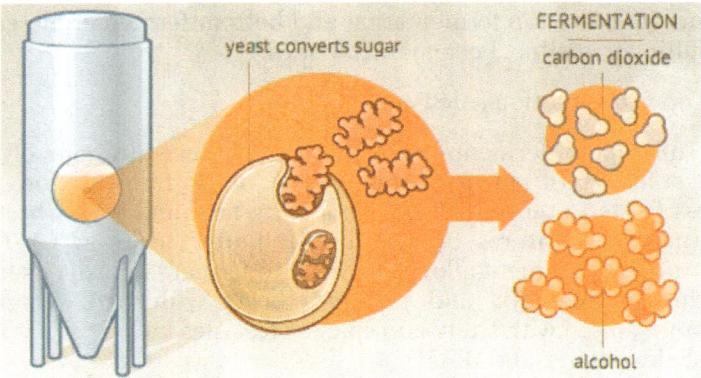

Fermentation is a delicate process that requires careful control of conditions like temperature and oxygen levels. Different strains of yeast and fermentation methods can lead to a wide variety of beer styles, from light and refreshing lagers to rich and complex ales.

Fermentation is the heart of beer making. It's the stage where simple ingredients are transformed into a flavourful, enjoyable beverage, thanks to the amazing work of tiny microorganisms.

1.2 Types of Fermentation in Beer Production

In beer production, fermentation isn't a one-size-fits-all process. There are different types of fermentation that brewers use to create the wide variety of beer styles we enjoy today. The main types are top fermentation and bottom fermentation, each resulting in distinct beer characteristics.

1. Top Fermentation (Ale Fermentation):

This type of fermentation is used to produce ales, one of the oldest and most popular types of beer. In top fermentation, the yeast floats to the top of the fermenting beer and works best at warmer temperatures, typically between 60-75°F (15-24°C). This warmer environment allows the yeast to ferment quickly, usually within a few days, and produces beers with rich, complex flavours, often with fruity and spicy notes. Ales include styles like pale ales, stouts, and IPAs.

2. Bottom Fermentation (Lager Fermentation):

Bottom fermentation is used to create lagers, which are known for their clean, crisp taste. In this process, the yeast settles at the bottom of the fermentation vessel and ferments at cooler temperatures, typically between 45-55°F (7-13°C). Because of the lower temperature, fermentation takes longer, sometimes several weeks. This slower, cooler fermentation process results in a smooth, refined beer with fewer fruity or spicy flavours. Popular lager styles include pilsners, bocks, and helles.

3. Spontaneous Fermentation:

Unlike the controlled processes of top and bottom fermentation, spontaneous fermentation relies on wild yeast and bacteria naturally present in the environment. This method is traditional in some Belgian beer styles, such as lambics. The beer is left exposed to the air, allowing these wild microorganisms to start the fermentation. The result is a beer with unique, often sour and funky flavours that are highly complex and unpredictable.

4. Mixed Fermentation:

Mixed fermentation combines elements of controlled yeast fermentation and spontaneous fermentation. Brewers might start with a top or bottom fermentation and then introduce wild yeasts or bacteria to create additional layers of flavour. This approach is often used in craft brewing to create innovative, complex beer styles that offer a balance of traditional and experimental flavours.

The type of fermentation used in beer production plays a crucial role in determining the beer's flavour, aroma, and overall style. Whether it's the quick, warm fermentation of ales or the slow, cool process of lagers, each type offers unique characteristics that contribute to the diversity of beers available today.

1.3 Ingredients in Fermentation: Yeast, Malt, Water, and Hops

Beer is made from four main ingredients, each playing a crucial role in the brewing process. Understanding these ingredients will help you appreciate the complexity and variety of flavours in different beers.

1. Yeast:

Yeast is a tiny microorganism that is essential for fermentation. It eats the sugars in the wort (the liquid extracted from malted grains) and turns them into alcohol and carbon dioxide. There are two main types of yeast used in brewing: ale yeast and lager yeast. Ale yeast works at warmer temperatures and produces beers with a range of fruity and spicy flavours, while lager yeast works at cooler temperatures and creates smoother, cleaner-tasting beers. Yeast also contributes to the aroma and complexity of the beer.

2. Malt:

Malt is made from barley grains that have been soaked, germinated, and then dried. This process, known as malting, develops the enzymes needed to convert the grains' starches into sugars during brewing. Malt gives beer its sweetness, body, and colour. Different types of malt can add various flavours, from the caramel notes in a brown ale to the rich, roasted flavours in a stout.

3. Water:

Water is the largest component of beer, making up the majority of its volume. The quality and mineral content of the water used can significantly affect the beer's taste and character. Different regions have distinct water profiles that influence the style of beer traditionally brewed there. For instance, the soft, mineral-rich waters of Dublin are ideal for stouts, while the hard waters of Burton-on-Trent are perfect for pale ales.

4. Hops:

Hops are the flowers of the hop plant, and they play multiple roles in beer. They add bitterness to balance the sweetness of the malt, making the beer taste more balanced and less cloying. Hops also contribute to the aroma and flavour, giving beers their distinctive notes, such as floral, citrusy, or piney. The timing and amount of hops added during brewing can influence how prominent these flavours become.

In summary, yeast, malt, water, and hops are the fundamental ingredients in beer, each contributing essential qualities to the final product. Yeast ferments the sugars, malt provides sweetness and body, water affects the overall taste, and hops add bitterness and aroma. Together, they create the wide range of beer styles and flavours we enjoy.

CHAPTER 2

THE BEER BREWING PROCESS

2.1 Overview of the Brewing Process

Brewing beer is a fascinating journey that transforms simple ingredients into a refreshing beverage. Here's a straightforward overview of the brewing process, breaking it down into key steps:

1. Malting:

The journey begins with malting, where grains, usually barley, are soaked in water to germinate. After germination, the grains are dried in a kiln. This process develops the enzymes needed to convert the grains' starches into sugars, which are crucial for fermentation.

2. Mashing:

The malted grains are then crushed and mixed with hot water in a process called mashing. This creates a thick, porridge-like mixture known as the mash. The heat activates the enzymes in the malt, which break down the starches into fermentable sugars. This results in a sweet liquid called wort.

3. Lautering

In the lautering stage, the wort is separated from the solid grain husks. The liquid wort is drained off, leaving behind the spent grains. The wort is then collected and often rinsed with hot water in a process called sparging to extract as much sugar as possible.

4. Boiling:

The wort is then boiled in a large kettle. During the boiling stage, hops are added to the wort. Hops contribute bitterness to balance the sweetness of the malt and also add flavours and aromas. The boiling process also helps to sterilize the wort and remove undesirable compounds.

5. Cooling:

After boiling, the hot wort needs to be cooled quickly to a temperature suitable for fermentation. This is typically done using a heat exchanger or a cooling coil. Rapid cooling is important to avoid any contamination and to ensure that the yeast will work effectively.

6. Fermentation:

The cooled wort is transferred to a fermentation vessel, where yeast is added. This is the fermentation stage, where the yeast consumes the sugars in the wort and produces alcohol and carbon dioxide. This stage can last from a few days to several weeks, depending on the type of beer being brewed.

7. Conditioning:

After fermentation, the beer is conditioned to develop its flavours and carbonation. This can be done in the fermentation vessel or in bottles and kegs. Conditioning allows the flavours to meld and any unwanted by-products to dissipate, resulting in a smoother, well-rounded beer.

8. Packaging:

Once conditioning is complete, the beer is packaged for consumption. It can be bottled, canned, or kegged. Packaging also includes adding any final carbonation if needed, and ensuring that the beer is properly sealed to maintain freshness.

The brewing process involves several key stages, from malting and mashing to fermentation and packaging. Each step is crucial for creating the final beer, with careful attention to detail ensuring that the beer turns out just right.

2.2 The Malting Process: From Grain to Malt

The malting process is a critical step in brewing beer, where raw grains are transformed into malt, the key ingredient that provides the sugars needed for fermentation. Here's a simple breakdown of how this process works:

1. Steeping:

The process begins with soaking the raw grains, typically barley, in water. This step is called steeping. The grains absorb the water and begin to sprout, which activates enzymes within them. These enzymes are essential for breaking down the starches in the grain into sugars later in the process.

2. Germination:

After steeping, the soaked grains are spread out in a controlled environment to allow them to germinate. This means the grains start to sprout tiny shoots. During germination, the enzymes in the grains break down the stored starches into simpler sugars. The sprouting grains are regularly turned to ensure even growth and prevent overheating.

3. Kilning:

Once germination is complete, the sprouted grains are dried in a kiln. This step is known as kilning. The drying process halts the germination and preserves the grains in their malted form. The temperature and duration of kilning can be adjusted to produce different types of malt, from pale malts to darker, richer malts. The heat also develops the flavours and colours of the malt.

4. Crushing:

After kilning, the malted grains are crushed or milled. This breaks them into smaller pieces, making it easier to extract the sugars during the mashing process. The crushed malt, now called grist, is ready to be mixed with water to create the mash, the next step in brewing.

The malting process transforms raw grains into malt through steeping, germination, kilning, and crushing. Each step is carefully controlled to develop the flavours, colours, and sugars that are essential for brewing beer.

2.3 Mashing and Lautering: Extracting Sugars

Mashing and lautering are essential stages in the brewing process where the goal is to extract fermentable sugars from malted grains, which will later be fermented by yeast to produce alcohol. These steps are crucial for determining the flavor, body, and strength of the final beer. Here's an in-depth look at how these processes work:

Mashing: Converting Starch to Sugar

Mashing is the process of mixing the crushed, malted grains (primarily barley) with hot water to activate the enzymes in the malt that convert starches into fermentable sugars. This is the first step in creating the wort, the liquid that will eventually become beer.

How Mashing Works:

- Crushed Malt: The malted barley (or other grains) is first milled or crushed to expose the inner starches while leaving the husk largely intact. The husks will later act as a filter bed during lautering.

- Water Addition: The crushed malt is mixed with water in a vessel known as a mash tun. The water temperature typically ranges from 145°F to 158°F (63°C to 70°C), depending on the type of beer being brewed.

- Enzyme Activation: The heat activates enzymes in the malt, primarily amylase enzymes, which break down the complex starches in the grain into simpler sugars like glucose and maltose. These sugars are essential for fermentation, as they are consumed by yeast to produce alcohol and carbon dioxide.

- ✓ Beta-amylase: Works best at lower temperatures (around 140°F to 150°F or 60°C to 65°C) and breaks starch into maltose, which is highly fermentable.
- ✓ Alpha-amylase: Works best at higher temperatures (around 154°F to 162°F or 68°C to 72°C) and breaks starch into more complex sugars that add body to the beer but are less fermentable.

- Time: The mash is typically allowed to rest for 60 to 90 minutes, giving the enzymes time to fully break down the starches.

Why It's Important:

Mashing determines the sugar content of the wort, which in turn affects the alcohol content and sweetness of the final beer. It also helps to develop some of the flavours and mouthfeel.

Lautering: Separating the Wort from the Grains

Lautering is the process that follows mashing, where the liquid wort is separated from the spent grains. This process involves draining and rinsing the grain bed to extract as much of the sugar-rich liquid as possible.

How Lautering Works:

- Mash Separation: After the mashing process, the mixture is transferred to a lautering tun, a vessel designed with a false bottom to help separate the liquid wort from the solid grains.
- First Runnings: The initial liquid that drains out, called the first wort, is usually the richest in sugars. This liquid is collected in a kettle or a holding vessel.
- Sparging: Once the first wort is drained, the grains are rinsed with hot water in a process called sparging. This helps to extract the remaining sugars still trapped in the grain bed. Sparging is usually done in two ways:
    - ✓ Fly sparging: Water is gently sprayed over the grain bed while the wort is continuously drained.
    - ✓ Batch sparging: Water is added in batches, and the wort is drained after each addition.
- Final Wort Collection: The wort collected after sparging is combined with the first wort, and together they make

up the total wort that will be boiled in the next step of brewing.

Why Lautering is Important:

Lautering ensures that the brewer extracts as much sugar as possible from the grains, maximizing efficiency. A well-executed lautering process leads to clear wort, which results in cleaner, more polished beer flavours.

Challenges in Mashing and Lautering

- Mash Temperature: The temperature during mashing is critical, as it affects the balance between fermentable and non-fermentable sugars. Too high a temperature can result in a less fermentable wort, leading to a sweeter beer, while too low a temperature can result in a thin, over-attenuated beer.
- Stuck Mash: In lautering, if the grain bed becomes too compacted, liquid cannot drain properly, leading to a "stuck mash." This can delay the brewing process and reduce sugar extraction.

The Importance of Mashing and Lautering in Beer Quality

Together, mashing and lautering determine much of the beer's final characteristics:

- Alcohol Content: The amount of fermentable sugar extracted in these processes impacts how much alcohol the yeast will be able to produce during fermentation.
- Flavour and Body: The balance between different sugars and the degree of sugar extraction influence not only the beer's flavour but also its mouthfeel and body.
- Efficiency: The more efficient the mashing and lautering processes, the more sugars are extracted, making the brewing process more cost-effective, especially on a larger scale.

Mashing and lautering are two critical steps in the brewing process that lay the foundation for the beer's flavour, strength, and overall quality. Mastering these stages is essential for any brewer, whether you're making beer at home or in a commercial brewery.

CHAPTER 3

THE ROLE OF YEAST IN BEER FERMENTATION

3.1 Types of Yeast Used in Brewing

Yeast is a tiny microorganism that plays a central role in brewing beer. It's responsible for fermentation, where it converts sugars into alcohol and carbon dioxide. There are different types of yeast used in brewing, each bringing unique characteristics to the beer. Here's a simple overview of the main types:

1. Ale Yeast (Saccharomyces cerevisiae):

Ale yeast is used for top fermentation. This type of yeast works best at warmer temperatures, typically between 60-75°F (15-24°C). When ale yeast ferments, it rises to the top of the fermentation vessel. It's known for producing a wide range of flavours and aromas, including fruity and spicy notes. This makes it ideal for creating diverse beer styles such as pale ales, IPAs, and stouts. Ale yeast tends to be quick and vigorous in its fermentation, often completing the process in a few days.

2. Lager Yeast (Saccharomyces pastorianus):

Lager yeast is used for bottom fermentation. It works best at cooler temperatures, usually between 45-55°F (7-13°C). Unlike ale yeast, lager yeast settles at the bottom of the fermentation vessel. This cooler fermentation process is slower, often taking several weeks. Lager yeast produces beers with a clean, crisp taste and fewer fruity or spicy flavours. It's commonly used for brewing lagers like pilsners, helles, and bocks.

3. Wild Yeast and Brettanomyces:

Wild yeast strains, including Brettanomyces, are used in some specialty and traditional beers. Brettanomyces can introduce unique, complex flavours such as earthy, fruity, or funky notes. These yeasts are often used in styles like lambics and sour ales. Wild yeast fermentation can be unpredictable and requires careful handling to ensure desired results.

4. Specialty Yeasts:

Brewers sometimes use specialty yeasts to create unique flavours or to adapt to specific brewing conditions. These can include yeast strains that produce higher alcohol content, or those that impart distinct flavours like spices or herbs. Specialty yeasts allow brewers to experiment and innovate, adding variety to the beer landscape.

The type of yeast used in brewing significantly impacts the flavour, aroma, and style of the beer. Ale yeasts offer a broad range of flavours and are used in warmer fermentation, while lager yeasts create clean, crisp beers through cooler fermentation. Wild and specialty yeasts introduce unique characteristics, making the world of beer rich and diverse.

3.2 Yeast Propagation and Maintenance

Yeast is a crucial ingredient in brewing, so managing it properly is key to producing high-quality beer. Yeast propagation and maintenance involve growing and caring for yeast to ensure it performs well during fermentation. Here's a straightforward explanation of these important processes:

1. Yeast Propagation:

Propagation is the process of growing yeast from a small quantity into a larger, healthy culture. This is often done using a starter. A yeast starter is a small batch of wort (the sugary liquid from malted grains) that is used to grow yeast before adding it to the main batch of beer. Here's how it works:

- Preparing the Starter: Mix a small amount of wort with yeast and allow it to ferment for a short time. This encourages the yeast to multiply and become more active.
- Growing the Culture: Once the starter has fermented, the yeast is added to the larger batch of wort. This ensures that there is enough healthy yeast to ferment the entire batch of beer effectively.

2. Yeast Maintenance:

Proper maintenance of yeast is essential to keep it healthy and effective for future batches. Here's what that involves:

- Storage: After fermentation, yeast can be collected and stored for future use. This is done by separating the yeast from the beer (known as yeast harvesting) and keeping it in a cool, sterile environment. Yeast should be stored at a low temperature to slow down its activity and prolong its viability.
- Sanitation: Keeping everything clean is crucial to prevent contamination. Contaminated yeast can lead to off-flavors or spoilage. Ensure that all equipment used in yeast handling is thoroughly sanitized.
- Yeast Viability: Before using stored yeast, check its viability. This can be done by preparing a small starter and observing how quickly it ferments. Healthy yeast will multiply and become active quickly, while old or weak yeast may not perform well.

3. Yeast Health:

Maintaining yeast health involves providing it with the right conditions to thrive:

- Proper Temperature: Yeast has an optimal temperature range for activity. Ensure that fermentation temperatures are within this range to avoid stressing the yeast.

- Nutrients: Yeast needs nutrients to grow and ferment effectively. These nutrients are usually present in the malt, but sometimes additional nutrients may be needed, especially in high-alcohol or complex recipes.

Yeast propagation and maintenance are key to successful brewing. Propagation involves growing a small amount of yeast into a larger, active culture, while maintenance focuses on storing and caring for yeast to keep it healthy and effective. Proper management ensures that your yeast performs well, leading to consistent and high-quality beer.

3.3 The Fermentation Process: Primary and Secondary Fermentation

Fermentation is the stage in beer brewing where sugars are converted into alcohol and carbon dioxide by yeast. This process is the heart of beer production and involves two main phases: primary fermentation and secondary fermentation. Each phase plays a vital role in developing the beer's flavour, aroma, and carbonation.

Primary Fermentation: The Initial Stage

Primary fermentation is the initial phase where yeast converts the majority of the fermentable sugars in the wort into alcohol and carbon dioxide. This process typically occurs in a fermentation vessel, such as a carboy or a fermentation tank, at a controlled temperature.

How Primary Fermentation Works:

- Pitching the Yeast: After the wort has been cooled to the appropriate fermentation temperature (usually between 60°F to 75°F or 15°C to 24°C for ales, and 45°F to 55°F or 7°C to 13°C for lagers), yeast is added. This step is called pitching the yeast.

- Active Fermentation: The yeast begins to consume the sugars (primarily glucose and maltose) in the wort. This process produces alcohol (ethanol) and carbon dioxide as by-products.

- ✓ Alcohol Production: The yeast metabolizes the sugars, generating ethanol, which gives the beer its alcohol content.
- ✓ Carbon Dioxide Production: The carbon dioxide (CO_2) is mostly released into the air, but some of it remains dissolved in the beer, contributing to its carbonation.

- Exothermic Reaction: Fermentation is an exothermic process, meaning it generates heat. This is why controlling the temperature during fermentation is crucial to prevent off-flavours.
- By-Products: In addition to alcohol and CO_2, yeast produces various other compounds such as esters, phenols, and fusel alcohols, which contribute to the flavour and aroma of the beer.
- Duration: Primary fermentation typically lasts between 3 to 10 days, depending on the yeast strain, fermentation temperature, and beer style. During this time, yeast is highly active, and the beer will appear cloudy due to suspended yeast cells.
- End of Primary Fermentation: You know primary fermentation is nearing completion when the bubbling in the airlock (if using one) slows down or stops. At this point, most of the sugars have been consumed, and the alcohol content has reached its desired level.

Secondary Fermentation: Conditioning and Maturation

Secondary fermentation is the phase after the primary fermentation, where the beer is conditioned and matured. This step is not always necessary but is often used to refine the beer, develop more complex flavours, and clarify the final product.

How Secondary Fermentation Works:

- Transfer to Secondary Vessel: Once primary fermentation is complete, the beer is often siphoned into a secondary fermenter. This vessel is usually smaller and is sealed to limit exposure to oxygen.

- Clarification: During secondary fermentation, the yeast and other solids (like hop particles and proteins) settle to the bottom, clarifying the beer. This results in a clearer final product, especially important for styles like lagers and pale ales.

- Flavour Development: While primary fermentation is focused on alcohol production, secondary fermentation allows for further flavour development. Esters and other by-products produced during fermentation can mature, adding complexity to the beer.

    ✓ Reduction of Off-Flavours: By allowing the beer to sit for an extended period, certain off-flavours (like diacetyl, which gives a buttery taste) can be reabsorbed by the yeast, resulting in a cleaner flavour profile.

- Carbonation: Although most carbonation happens during primary fermentation; some brewers use secondary fermentation to naturally carbonate the beer. This can be done by adding a small amount of sugar to the beer before sealing it in bottles or kegs (called bottle conditioning or keg conditioning).

- Duration: Secondary fermentation can last anywhere from a few days to several months, depending on the beer style. Lighter ales may require only a few days or weeks, while stronger beers or those with more complex flavours (such as Belgian ales or stouts) may benefit from a longer maturation period.

Differences Between Primary and Secondary Fermentation

i. Primary Fermentation:

- Main Purpose: Conversion of sugars into alcohol and carbon dioxide.

- Activity: Highly active phase with visible yeast activity (bubbling and foaming).

- Time Frame: Shorter duration (3 to 10 days).

- Result: Most of the alcohol content is produced, but the beer is still raw and needs conditioning.

ii. Secondary Fermentation:

- Main Purpose: Conditioning, clarifying, and maturing the beer.
- Activity: Less visible activity as yeast cells settle and flavours develop.
- Time Frame: Longer duration (weeks to months).
- Result: Refined flavours, clearer appearance, and a more polished final product.

The Importance of Temperature Control in Both Phases

- Primary Fermentation Temperature: If the temperature is too high, yeast may produce off-flavours, such as fruity esters or harsh fusel alcohols. If the temperature is too low, yeast activity may slow down, leading to incomplete fermentation.
- Secondary Fermentation Temperature: For secondary fermentation, a cooler temperature is often preferred (around 50°F to 60°F or 10°C to 15°C), which allows the beer to mature without producing unwanted flavours.

When to Use Secondary Fermentation

Not all beers require secondary fermentation. Lighter ales, pale ales, and beers meant to be consumed quickly (such as wheat beers) may skip secondary fermentation altogether and be bottled or kegged directly after primary fermentation. However, for more complex beers like stouts, porters, and high-gravity brews, secondary fermentation helps to smooth out the flavours and improve the beer's overall quality.

Common Issues During Fermentation

- Stuck Fermentation: Sometimes, yeast may stop fermenting before all the sugars have been converted. This is called a stuck fermentation and can result from factors like insufficient nutrients, poor yeast health, or incorrect fermentation temperatures.
- Off-Flavours: Improper temperature control or poor yeast management during either phase can lead to

undesirable flavours in the final beer, such as sulphur, diacetyl, or excessive ester production.

Primary and secondary fermentation are key steps in the brewing process that shape the character of the beer. The primary phase focuses on alcohol production, while the secondary phase allows for refinement, maturation, and the development of more complex flavours. Mastering these fermentation stages ensures a balanced, flavourful, and high-quality beer.

CHAPTER 4

FERMENTATION EQUIPMENT AND SETUP

4.1 Essential Equipment for Home Brewing

Brewing beer at home is a fun and rewarding hobby, but it requires some basic equipment to get started. Here's a straightforward guide to the essential tools and supplies you'll need for home brewing:

1. Brewing Kettle:

The brewing kettle is where you'll boil the wort, which is the sugary liquid extracted from the malted grains. It's typically a large pot made of stainless steel or aluminium, and it should be big enough to hold the wort and allow for boiling. A kettle with a spigot for easy pouring is also helpful.

2. Fermentation Vessel:

This is where the wort will ferment once you've added yeast. Common options include glass carboys, plastic buckets, or food-grade plastic fermenters. It's important to use a vessel with an airlock to let carbon dioxide escape while keeping contaminants out.

3. Airlock:

An airlock is a small device that fits into the top of the fermentation vessel. It allows gases to escape during fermentation without letting outside air or contaminants enter. This helps prevent spoilage and ensures a healthy fermentation process.

4. Hydrometer:

A hydrometer measures the specific gravity (density) of the wort, which helps you track the fermentation progress and determine the final alcohol content. It's a useful tool for monitoring how much sugar has been converted into alcohol.

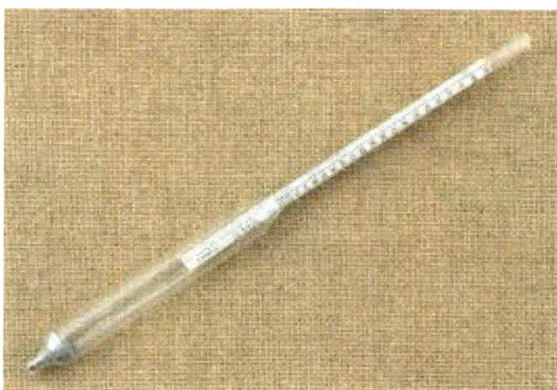

5. Siphon or Auto-Siphon:

A siphon is used to transfer beer from one container to another without disturbing the sediment at the bottom. An auto-siphon makes this process easier by using a pump to start the flow of liquid.

6. Sanitizer:

Sanitation is crucial in brewing to prevent infections and off-flavours. Use a food-safe sanitizer to clean and disinfect all your equipment before and after use. This helps ensure that your beer turns out as intended.

7. Brewing Spoon:

A long-handled spoon, preferably made of stainless steel or food-grade plastic, is used for stirring the wort during brewing. It's essential for mixing ingredients and preventing scorching.

8. Thermometer:

A thermometer helps you monitor the temperature of the wort and fermentation. Accurate temperature control is important for achieving the desired flavour and fermentation results.

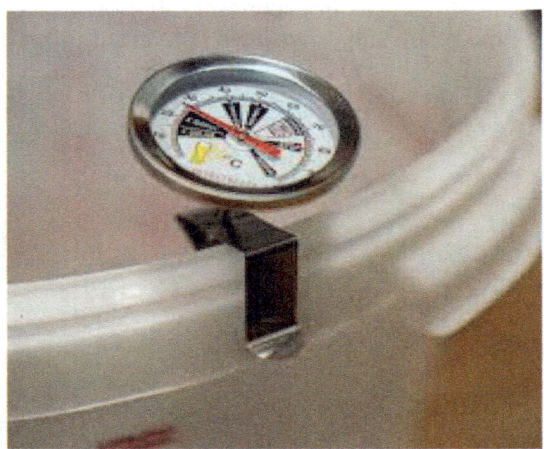

9. Bottles or Kegs:

Once fermentation is complete, you'll need a way to package your beer. You can use bottles with caps or kegs for larger batches. If using bottles, you'll also need a bottle capper and caps to seal them.

10. Bottle Brush:

A bottle brush is used to clean the inside of bottles. Keeping bottles clean and free of residue is important to ensure your beer remains fresh and free from contamination.

The essential equipment for home brewing includes a brewing kettle, fermentation vessel, airlock, hydrometer, siphon, sanitizer, brewing spoon, thermometer, and packaging options like bottles or kegs. With these tools, you'll be well-equipped to start brewing your own delicious beer at home.

4.2 Setting Up a Fermentation Space

Setting up a good fermentation space is crucial for successful home brewing. The right environment ensures that your beer ferments properly, leading to the best possible flavour and quality. Here's a simple guide to help you create an ideal fermentation space:

1. Choose the Right Location:

Select a space that is cool, dark, and clean. Fermentation can be sensitive to light and temperature, so avoid placing your fermentation vessel in direct sunlight or near heat sources. A basement, closet, or pantry is often a good choice.

2. Temperature Control:

Maintaining a consistent temperature is important for fermentation. Different yeast strains have optimal temperature ranges, so ensure your fermentation space can stay within these limits. For ales, a temperature range of 60-75°F (15-24°C) is typically ideal. For lagers, a cooler range of 45-55°F (7-13°C) is needed. You might use a temperature-controlled space or an old refrigerator with a temperature controller to keep conditions stable.

3. Cleanliness:

Keep your fermentation space clean and free from contaminants. This helps prevent infections and off-flavours in your beer. Regularly clean and sanitize the area where you'll be handling your fermentation equipment.

4. Airflow:

Ensure there is good airflow around your fermentation vessel. This helps dissipate heat produced during fermentation and prevents the build up of unwanted odours. Avoid overcrowding the space to allow proper ventilation.

5. Accessibility:

Set up your fermentation space in a location that's easily accessible. You'll need to check on your fermentation regularly, so choose a spot where you can easily monitor and manage your brewing process.

6. Storage for Equipment:

Organize your brewing equipment and supplies in a way that's convenient and easy to access. Use shelves, bins, or cabinets to keep everything tidy and within reach.

7. Safety:

Ensure that the area is safe and free from hazards. Avoid placing heavy items above your fermentation vessel to prevent accidents. Also, keep any cleaning supplies or chemicals away from your brewing area.

8. Temperature Monitoring:

Consider using a thermometer or a temperature probe to keep track of the temperature of your fermentation vessel. This helps you ensure that the temperature remains within the ideal range for your yeast.

Setting up a fermentation space involves choosing a cool, dark, and clean location with good temperature control and airflow. Keep the area organized and accessible, and ensure it's safe and suitable for monitoring your brewing process. With the right setup, your fermentation will go smoothly, leading to delicious homemade beer.

4.3 Sanitization and Cleanliness in Brewing

Sanitization and cleanliness are crucial for brewing beer at home. Properly cleaning and sanitizing your equipment helps ensure that your beer turns out great and is free from unwanted flavours or contamination. Here's a simple guide to keep your brewing process clean and effective:

1. Why Cleanliness Matters:

Keeping everything clean is essential because any dirt, bacteria, or residue can spoil your beer. Contaminants can introduce off-flavors, unwanted bacteria, or even make your beer unsafe to drink. Cleanliness helps ensure that your beer tastes as good as it should and is safe to enjoy.

2. Cleaning vs. Sanitizing:

Cleaning and sanitizing are two different steps:

- Cleaning: This involves removing visible dirt and residue from your equipment. Use warm, soapy water and a scrub brush or sponge to clean your brewing tools, fermenters, and bottles. Make sure to clean all surfaces thoroughly, including those that come into contact with your beer.

- Sanitizing: After cleaning, sanitizing kills any remaining microorganisms that could spoil your beer. Use a food-safe sanitizer designed for brewing equipment. Follow the manufacturer's instructions for mixing and contact time to ensure effective sanitization.

3. Cleaning Equipment:

Before each use, clean all your brewing equipment, including:

- Brewing Kettle: Wash and rinse it thoroughly after each use.

- Fermentation Vessel: Clean the inside and outside, paying attention to any residue or sediment.

- Siphon and Tubing: Clean and sanitize these parts to avoid contamination during transfers.

- Bottles and Caps: Clean bottles thoroughly before filling them with beer, and sanitize them to prevent spoilage.

4. Sanitizing Process:

To properly sanitize your equipment:

- Prepare the Sanitizer: Mix the sanitizer according to the instructions on the packaging. Ensure it's at the correct concentration and temperature.

- Apply the Sanitizer: Pour or spray the sanitizer onto all equipment, ensuring every surface is covered.

- Contact Time: Allow the sanitizer to sit for the recommended time to effectively kill microorganisms. Avoid rinsing unless instructed to do so.

- Air Dry: Let the equipment air dry in a clean, dust-free environment. Avoid touching sanitized surfaces with your hands or placing them on unclean surfaces.

5. Regular Maintenance:

Keep your brewing area and equipment clean between brewing sessions. Regularly clean and sanitize your equipment even if you're not brewing immediately. This prevents any build up of residues or contaminants.

6. Personal Hygiene:

Practice good personal hygiene when brewing. Wash your hands thoroughly before handling any equipment or ingredients. This helps prevent transferring any unwanted microbes into your brewing setup.

Proper sanitization and cleanliness are vital for successful home brewing. Clean all equipment thoroughly to remove dirt and residue, then sanitize to kill any remaining microorganisms. Keeping your brewing area and equipment clean ensures your beer is delicious, safe, and free from contamination.

CHAPTER 5

CONTROLLING FERMENTATION VARIABLES

5.1 Temperature Control During Fermentation

Temperature control is a key factor in brewing great beer. The temperature at which fermentation takes place affects the yeast's activity and the overall quality of your beer. Here's a simple guide to understanding and managing temperature during fermentation:

1. Why Temperature Matters:

Yeast is sensitive to temperature changes, and different yeast strains have specific temperature ranges where they perform best. The right temperature ensures that the yeast ferments the sugars in your wort efficiently, leading to better flavour and fewer off-flavors.

2. Ideal Temperature Ranges:

- Ale Yeast: Typically thrives at warmer temperatures between 60-75°F (15-24°C). This range allows ale yeast to ferment quickly and develop a variety of flavors.
- Lager Yeast: Prefers cooler temperatures, usually between 45-55°F (7-13°C). This slower fermentation process helps lager yeast produce clean, crisp flavors.
- Wild and Specialty Yeasts: These can have varying temperature needs, often listed in the yeast's specific guidelines.

3. Maintaining Consistent Temperature:

Fermentation temperature can fluctuate due to changes in room temperature or other factors. To maintain a stable temperature:

- Fermentation Chamber: Use a dedicated fermentation chamber or an old refrigerator with a temperature controller to keep the temperature consistent. This setup is especially useful for lagering or when precise temperature control is needed.
- Temperature Belts or Pads: These devices wrap around your fermentation vessel and help regulate temperature by either heating or cooling it.
- Insulation: Insulating your fermentation vessel can help maintain a steady temperature and protect against external temperature changes. Use materials like foam or blankets designed for insulation.

4. Monitoring Temperature:

Regularly check the temperature of your fermentation vessel:

- Thermometer: Use a thermometer to monitor the temperature of your beer. Some fermenters have built-in temperature gauges, but an external thermometer or temperature probe can also be useful.

- Thermometer Strips: Adhesive thermometer strips can be attached to the outside of your fermentation vessel to give a quick and easy temperature reading.

5. Temperature Variations:

Avoid large temperature swings, as they can stress the yeast and lead to undesirable flavors or stalled fermentation. Keep your fermentation space as stable as possible, and make adjustments gradually if you need to change the temperature.

6. Post-Fermentation:

After fermentation is complete, it's often beneficial to allow your beer to condition at a stable temperature. This maturation phase can improve flavour and clarity.

Controlling the temperature during fermentation is crucial for brewing high-quality beer. Maintain a consistent temperature within the ideal range for your yeast strain to ensure a smooth fermentation process and to achieve the best flavour and quality in your beer.

5.2 Monitoring and Adjusting pH Levels

Monitoring and adjusting pH levels is an important aspect of brewing that can influence the taste, clarity, and overall quality of your beer. Here's a simple guide to understanding and managing pH levels in your brewing process:

1. What is pH?

pH measures the acidity or alkalinity of a liquid. In brewing, it affects enzyme activity during mashing and the flavour of the finished beer. The pH scale ranges from 0 (very acidic) to 14 (very alkaline), with 7 being neutral.

2. Ideal pH Levels for Brewing:

- Mashing: The pH during mashing should typically be between 5.2 and 5.6. This range ensures that enzymes can efficiently convert starches into sugars.

- Boiling: The pH during boiling should be around 5.0 to 5.5. This helps with hop utilization and prevents excessive bitterness.

- Fermentation: The pH of the wort before fermentation should be in the 5.2 to 5.6 range, but it will naturally drop as fermentation progresses due to the production of organic acids by the yeast.

3. Monitoring pH Levels:

- pH Meter: A pH meter is a precise tool for measuring the acidity of your wort or beer. Follow the manufacturer's instructions for calibration and use to get accurate readings.

- pH Strips: pH strips are a more affordable option for checking pH levels. They are less precise than a meter but can still provide useful information.

4. Adjusting pH Levels:

If you find that the pH is outside the ideal range, you may need to make adjustments:

- During Mashing: Add acid malt, lactic acid, or phosphoric acid to lower the pH. Conversely, you can use baking soda to raise the pH if it's too low.

- During Boiling: Similar to mashing, you can adjust the pH by adding acids or bases, depending on whether you need to lower or raise the pH.

- During Fermentation: pH naturally drops as fermentation progresses. However, if you need to adjust the pH during fermentation, use food-grade acids or bases cautiously, as the yeast is actively working and sensitive to changes.

5. Impact of pH on Beer Quality:

- Flavour: pH affects the taste of your beer. A pH that is too high or too low can lead to off-flavors or harsh tastes.

- Clarity: Proper pH helps with protein-polyphenol interactions that affect clarity. A well-balanced pH can lead to clearer beer.

- Enzyme Activity: The right pH ensures that enzymes in the malt work efficiently, affecting the sugar extraction and overall fermentation process.

6. Regular Testing:

Incorporate regular pH testing into your brewing routine, especially during mashing and boiling, to maintain control over the brewing process and ensure consistent results.

Monitoring and adjusting pH levels are essential for brewing high-quality beer. Keeping pH levels within the ideal ranges for mashing, boiling, and fermentation helps achieve the best flavour, clarity, and efficiency in your brewing process.

5.3 Oxygen Management in Fermentation

Oxygen management is crucial for brewing beer, as it affects the fermentation process and the final quality of your beer. Here's a simple guide to understanding and managing oxygen during fermentation:

1. Why Oxygen Matters:

Oxygen plays a key role in the brewing process, but its impact varies depending on the stage of brewing:

- Before Fermentation: When you first pitch yeast into your wort, a small amount of oxygen is beneficial. It helps yeast grow and multiply, leading to a healthy fermentation. However, too much oxygen at this stage can lead to off-flavors and spoilage.

- During and After Fermentation: Once fermentation begins, excess oxygen can be harmful. It can lead to oxidation, which can cause stale or cardboard-like flavors in your beer.

2. Managing Oxygen Levels:

- Aerating the Wort: Before you add yeast, it's important to aerate your wort to provide the yeast with the oxygen it needs. This can be done by shaking the fermenter vigorously or using an aquarium pump with an aeration stone to introduce oxygen. This step helps the yeast grow and start fermentation effectively.

- Minimizing Oxygen Exposure: After pitching the yeast, minimize oxygen exposure to avoid oxidation. This can be achieved by:
  - ✓ Sealing the Fermentation Vessel: Use an airlock or a similar device to keep the fermentation vessel sealed. This allows gases to escape while preventing outside air from entering.
  - ✓ Avoiding Excessive Agitation: Once fermentation has started, avoid stirring or shaking the fermenter, as this can introduce unwanted oxygen.
  - ✓ Using a Closed System: If possible, use a closed fermentation system that limits the amount of air that comes into contact with the beer. This is particularly important for sensitive styles and high-quality brews.

3. Post-Fermentation Oxygen Management:
   - When Bottling or Kegging: Oxygen can be introduced when transferring beer from the fermenter to bottles or kegs. To minimize oxygen pickup:
     - ✓ Use a Siphon or Auto-Siphon: Carefully siphon beer from the fermenter to avoid splashing or introducing air.
     - ✓ Fill Bottles or Kegs Properly: Fill bottles or kegs to the top to reduce the headspace, which minimizes the amount of oxygen trapped in the container.
   - Cap or Seal Immediately: Once bottles are filled or kegs are sealed, cap or seal them right away to prevent oxygen from getting in.

4. Monitoring for Oxidation:
   - Flavour Changes: Be aware of potential oxidation signs in your finished beer, such as off-flavors or a cardboard-like taste. If you notice these, it may indicate that oxygen

management needs improvement in your brewing process.

5. Best Practices:

- Clean and Sanitize: Ensure all equipment is properly cleaned and sanitized to avoid contamination that can be exacerbated by oxygen.
- Careful Handling: Handle your beer gently during transfers and bottling to minimize oxygen exposure.

Effective oxygen management in brewing involves aerating the wort before fermentation, minimizing oxygen exposure during and after fermentation, and careful handling when bottling or kegging. By managing oxygen levels carefully, you can help ensure that your beer tastes fresh and high-quality.

CHAPTER 6

Beer Styles and Fermentation Profiles

6.1 Ales: Fermentation Characteristics and Styles

Ales are one of the most popular and diverse types of beer, known for their wide range of flavors and aromas. Here's an easy-to-understand guide to what makes ales unique and the different styles you might encounter:

1. What are Ales?

Ales are a type of beer made using top-fermenting yeast, typically Saccharomyces cerevisiae. This yeast ferments at warmer temperatures, usually between 60-75°F (15-24°C). The result is a beer with a distinct character, often with more pronounced flavors and aromas compared to other beer types.

2. Fermentation Characteristics:

- Yeast: Ales use top-fermenting yeast, which means the yeast rises to the top of the fermenter during fermentation. This yeast works well at warmer temperatures, contributing to the ale's unique flavour profile.

- Temperature: The warmer fermentation temperatures of ales (compared to lagers) allow the yeast to produce a range of flavors, including fruity and spicy notes. This is why ales often have more complex aromas and flavors.

- Fermentation Time: Ales typically ferment faster than lagers. Primary fermentation can take a week or two, while secondary fermentation or conditioning might take additional time depending on the style.

3. Common Ale Styles:

Ales come in many styles, each with its own flavour profile and characteristics. Here are a few popular ones:

- Pale Ale: This style is known for its balanced flavour, with moderate hop bitterness and a clean, malty backbone. Variants include American Pale Ale (APA) and English Pale Ale.

- India Pale Ale (IPA): IPAs are hop-forward beers with a strong hop aroma and flavour. They can be bitter and may have notes of citrus, pine, or floral. Variants include American IPA, Double IPA, and New England IPA.

- Stout: Stouts are dark ales with roasted malt flavors. They can range from dry and coffee-like to rich and sweet, with flavors of chocolate, coffee, and caramel.

- Porter: Similar to stouts but generally lighter in body and less intense in flavour. Porters often have roasted malt flavors with notes of chocolate and coffee.

- Belgian Ale: This style encompasses a variety of beers with unique flavors due to the Belgian yeast strains used. Examples include Belgian Dubbel (rich and malty), Belgian Trippel (strong and fruity), and Belgian Witbier (spicy and refreshing with added spices and citrus peels).

- Saison: Also known as farmhouse ales, Saisons are known for their spicy, fruity flavors and dry finish. They often have a complex aroma and can include a variety of additional ingredients like herbs and spices.

4. Brewing Ales:

- Ingredients: Ales are brewed with malted barley, hops, water, and ale yeast. The choice of malt and hops can significantly impact the flavour profile.

- Process: Start by mashing the malted barley to extract sugars, boil the wort with hops, and then ferment with ale yeast at a warmer temperature. The fermentation process for ales is typically quicker than for lagers.

- Aging: While ales can be enjoyed relatively young, some styles, like strong ales or barrel-aged variants, benefit from additional aging to develop their full flavors.

5. Enjoying Ales:

- Glassware: Use appropriate glassware to enhance the aroma and flavour of your ale. For example, a tulip glass works well for IPAs and Belgian ales, while a pint glass is great for pale ales and stouts.

- Serving Temperature: Ales are often best enjoyed at slightly warmer temperatures than lagers. For most ales, serving them slightly chilled to room temperature can bring out the best flavors.

Ales are a diverse and flavourful category of beer, known for their use of top-fermenting yeast and warmer fermentation temperatures. With styles ranging from hoppy IPAs to rich stouts and complex Belgian ales, there's an ale for every taste preference. Understanding these characteristics can help you appreciate and choose the right ale for any occasion.

6.2 Lagers: Cold Fermentation and Maturation

Lagers are a popular type of beer known for their clean, crisp flavors and smooth finish. Here's a straightforward guide to understanding what makes lagers unique and how the cold fermentation and maturation processes contribute to their distinct characteristics:

1. What are Lagers?

Lagers are a type of beer that uses bottom-fermenting yeast, typically Saccharomyces pastorianus. This yeast ferments at cooler temperatures compared to ales, which results in a beer with a clean and smooth profile. The name "lager" comes from the German word "lagern," meaning "to store," reflecting the process of aging or maturing the beer.

2. Cold Fermentation:

- Yeast: Lagers use bottom-fermenting yeast that works best at cooler temperatures, generally between 45-55°F (7-13°C). This yeast settles at the bottom of the fermenter and ferments more slowly.

- Temperature: The cooler fermentation temperatures reduce the production of fruity and spicy esters, leading to a cleaner taste. This contrasts with ales, which are fermented at warmer temperatures and have more pronounced flavors.

- Fermentation Time: Lager fermentation typically takes longer than ale fermentation. Primary fermentation can last from several weeks to a couple of months, depending on the beer style and desired characteristics.

3. Maturation (Lagering):

- What is Maturation? After the initial fermentation, lagers undergo a maturation period known as "lagering." This involves storing the beer at near-freezing temperatures for several weeks or months.

- Purpose: Maturation allows flavors to meld and any unwanted compounds to be removed. It helps the beer achieve a smooth, clean taste and clarity.

- Process: During maturation, the beer undergoes secondary fermentation where additional yeast activity helps to further clarify the beer and refine its flavour. This process can also help to mellow any harsh or strong flavors from the initial fermentation.

4. Common Lager Styles:

Lagers come in various styles, each with its own flavour profile:

- Pale Lager: This is the most common type of lager, known for its light colour, mild flavour, and crisp finish. Examples include Pilsner and Helles.

- Pilsner: A type of pale lager with a distinct hop bitterness and floral aroma. It originates from the Czech Republic and Germany.

- Helles: A German pale lager that is slightly maltier and less hoppy than a Pilsner. It has a smooth, balanced flavour.

- Darker Lagers: Styles like Dunkel and Schwarzbier are darker lagers with richer, maltier flavors. Dunkel has notes of caramel and toffee, while Schwarzbier is known for its roasted malt flavors.

5. Brewing Lagers:

- Ingredients: Like ales, lagers are brewed with malted barley, hops, water, and yeast. The choice of malt and hops affects the flavour, but the key difference is the yeast and fermentation temperature.

- Process: Start by mashing the malted barley to extract sugars, boil the wort with hops, and then ferment with lager yeast at cool temperatures. After primary fermentation, transfer the beer to a secondary vessel for maturation.

- Aging: Allow the beer to age in a cold environment to develop its clean, crisp character. The aging process helps improve clarity and smoothness.

6. Enjoying Lagers:

- Glassware: Use a glass that highlights the beer's clarity and carbonation. A pilsner glass or a stein is ideal for many lager styles.

- Serving Temperature: Lagers are typically best served cold, around 45-50°F (7-10°C). This enhances their refreshing qualities and crisp finish.

Lagers are distinguished by their use of bottom-fermenting yeast and cold fermentation, resulting in a clean and smooth beer. The lagering process further refines the beer, allowing flavors to mature and develop clarity. With styles ranging from light and crisp pale lagers to rich and malty dark lagers, there's a lager for every taste preference.

6.3 Specialty Beers: Sours, Stouts, and Beyond

Specialty beers are a diverse group that includes unique styles with distinct flavors and brewing techniques. This category encompasses a wide range of beers, from tart and tangy sours to rich and complex stouts. Here's an easy-to-understand guide to some of the most popular specialty beer styles:

1. Sours:

Sour beers are known for their tart, acidic flavors, which result from wild yeast and bacteria used in their fermentation. These microorganisms produce lactic acid and other compounds that give the beer its characteristic sour taste.

Types of Sours:

- Berliner Weisse: A German-style sour wheat beer that is light, refreshing, and mildly sour. It often has fruity or herbal flavors and is sometimes served with flavoured syrups.

- **Gose:** A German-style sour ale that is both sour and salty. It's brewed with coriander and salt, giving it a unique flavour profile with tangy, salty notes.

- **Lambic:** A traditional Belgian sour beer made using spontaneous fermentation with wild yeasts and bacteria from the environment. It's often aged in barrels and can include fruit additions, like cherries or raspberries, to create complex, fruity flavors.

2. Stouts:

Stouts are dark beers known for their rich, roasted malt flavors. They often have notes of coffee, chocolate, and caramel. The dark colour comes from the use of roasted barley or malt.

Types of Stouts:

- **Dry Stout:** Known for its dry, roasted flavour, with notes of coffee and chocolate. The most famous example is Guinness.

- **Sweet Stout:** Also known as milk stout, this style includes lactose (milk sugar) which adds sweetness and creaminess to balance the roasted flavors.

- **Imperial Stout:** A stronger, higher-alcohol version of stouts with intense flavors of roasted malt, coffee, and chocolate. It often has a higher bitterness and complex flavour profile.

3. Other Specialty Beers:

i. Barrel-Aged Beers: These beers are aged in barrels that previously held spirits, wine, or other beverages. The aging process imparts additional flavors from the barrel, such as vanilla, oak, or whisky notes. Examples include bourbon barrel-aged stouts or wine barrel-aged sours.

ii. Spiced and Flavoured Beers: These beers include additional ingredients like spices, herbs, fruit, or other flavourings to create unique profiles. Examples include pumpkin ales with spices for fall or fruit-infused IPAs.

iii. Seasonal Beers: Often brewed to celebrate specific times of the year or holidays. Examples include Oktoberfest beers for fall and Christmas ales with festive spices.

4. Brewing Specialty Beers:

- Ingredients: Specialty beers often use unconventional ingredients or brewing methods. For sours, this might include wild yeast and bacteria. For stouts, roasted malts and adjuncts like coffee or chocolate are common.

- Process: The brewing process for specialty beers can vary widely. Sours often involve extended fermentation and aging. Stouts may include additional flavourings added during brewing or aging.

- Aging: Some specialty beers benefit from aging, which can enhance their flavors. This is especially true for barrel-aged beers and certain stouts that develop richer flavors over time.

5. Enjoying Specialty Beers:

- Glassware: Choose a glass that complements the beer style. For example, use a tulip glass for stouts to capture their rich aromas, or a fluted glass for sours to highlight their effervescence.

- Serving Temperature: Specialty beers can vary in serving temperature. Generally, stouts are served slightly warmer to enhance their flavors, while sours are best enjoyed chilled.

Specialty beers like sours and stouts offer a wide range of unique and flavourful experiences. Sours are known for their tangy and refreshing qualities, while stouts are rich and robust. Exploring these styles can introduce you to a world of complex and interesting flavors, perfect for those looking to try something beyond the standard beer offerings.

CHAPTER 7

PACKAGING AND CARBONATION

7.1 Bottling vs. Kegging: Pros and Cons

When it comes to packaging your homemade beer, you have two main options: bottling or kegging. Both methods have their advantages and disadvantages, so it's important to understand what each involves to choose the best one for your needs. Here's a straightforward guide to the pros and cons of bottling and kegging:

1. Bottling:

Pros:

- Cost-Effective: Bottling requires less initial investment. You only need bottles, caps, and a capping tool, which are relatively inexpensive compared to kegs and kegging equipment.

- Portability: Bottles are easy to take along to gatherings or share with friends. They are also convenient for small batches or personal use.

- Variety: Bottling allows you to package different beers in different styles of bottles (e.g., 12 oz, 22 oz, or 750 ml) and to use labels for personalization or branding.

- No Need for CO2: Bottles don't require a CO2 system to carbonate the beer, as carbonation is achieved through natural fermentation or priming sugar added before bottling.

Cons:

- Time-Consuming: The bottling process can be labour-intensive and time-consuming. You need to clean, sanitize, fill, and cap each bottle individually.

- Consistency Issues: Achieving consistent carbonation levels can be challenging. Bottles may vary slightly in carbonation, especially if priming sugar isn't evenly distributed.

- Storage Space: Bottles take up more storage space compared to kegs. You need a place to store the bottles both before and after they're filled.

- Potential for Infection: There's a risk of contamination if bottles aren't properly cleaned and sanitized. This can lead to off-flavors or spoilage.

2. Kegging:

Pros:

- Convenience: Kegging is more efficient for dispensing larger quantities of beer. Once the keg is set up, you can easily pour a draft beer without the need for individual bottle handling.

- Consistent Carbonation: Kegging allows for better control over carbonation levels. You can adjust the pressure on the CO_2 system to achieve consistent carbonation throughout the keg.

- Less Labour: The process of kegging involves fewer steps compared to bottling. Once the beer is transferred to the keg, you simply need to carbonate and dispense.

- Reduced Oxygen Exposure: Kegs minimize oxygen exposure compared to bottles, which can help preserve the beer's freshness and flavour for longer.

Cons:

- Initial Cost: Kegging equipment, including kegs, a CO_2 tank, regulator, and a dispensing system, can be expensive. There's also a need for a kegerator or suitable cooling system.

- Bulk Storage: Kegs take up more space and require a dedicated area for storage, such as a kegerator or refrigerator.

- Cleaning and Maintenance: Kegs need regular cleaning and maintenance to prevent contamination and ensure proper function. This includes cleaning lines and checking seals.

- Limited Portability: Kegs are less portable than bottles, making them less convenient for events or sharing with friends outside your home.

In Summary:

- Bottling is cost-effective and versatile, ideal for small batches or personal use, but it can be labour-intensive and may require careful attention to consistency and sanitation.

- Kegging is more convenient for dispensing larger quantities, provides consistent carbonation, and minimizes oxygen exposure, but it involves a higher initial investment and requires more space and maintenance.

Choosing between bottling and kegging depends on your brewing scale, budget, and preferences. Both methods can produce great beer; it's all about finding what works best for you and your brewing setup.

7.2 Carbonation Methods: Natural vs. Forced

Carbonation gives beer its refreshing fizz and effervescence. There are two main methods for achieving carbonation: natural carbonation and forced carbonation. Each method has its own set of benefits and considerations. Here's an easy-to-understand guide to help you decide which method suits your needs:

1. Natural Carbonation:

Natural carbonation occurs when carbon dioxide (CO_2) is produced through the fermentation process or by adding a small amount of sugar before bottling.

How It Works:

- Fermentation: During the primary fermentation, yeast consumes sugars and produces CO_2 as a by product. For natural carbonation, additional sugar (priming sugar) is added to the beer just before bottling. This sugar provides the yeast with extra food, leading to more CO_2 production and carbonation in the sealed bottles.

- Priming Sugar: The amount of sugar added before bottling is crucial. Too much can lead to over-carbonation and potentially burst bottles, while too little may result in flat beer. The sugar is usually in the form of dextrose or corn sugar.

Pros:

- No Additional Equipment: Natural carbonation doesn't require specialized equipment beyond what you already use for bottling. It's an economical method, as it relies on the yeast's natural process.

- Improved Flavors: Some brewers believe that natural carbonation can enhance the beer's flavour and mouthfeel, as the process of carbonation occurs slowly and naturally.

Cons:

- Time-Consuming: Natural carbonation takes time. After bottling, you'll need to wait several weeks for the beer to carbonate properly, which can delay the enjoyment of your brew.

- Consistency Issues: Achieving consistent carbonation levels can be challenging. Variations in temperature, sugar distribution, and yeast activity can result in inconsistent carbonation across bottles.

2. Forced Carbonation:

Forced carbonation involves adding CO_2 directly to the beer using a pressurized system, typically in a keg. This method provides precise control over the carbonation level.

How It Works:

- CO_2 Tank and Regulator: In a forced carbonation setup, you use a CO_2 tank connected to a regulator, which controls the amount of CO_2 being added to the beer. The beer is placed in a keg, and CO_2 is introduced under pressure.

- Carbonation Time: You can carbonate beer quickly with this method. Depending on the pressure and temperature, beer can be carbonated in a matter of hours to days.

Pros:

- Control: Forced carbonation allows precise control over carbonation levels. You can adjust the CO_2 pressure to achieve the desired fizz and consistency.

- Speed: You can carbonate beer much faster compared to natural carbonation. This is ideal if you're eager to enjoy

your brew sooner or need to carbonate large batches quickly.
- Consistency: Forced carbonation provides uniform carbonation throughout the keg, eliminating the variability found in natural carbonation.

Cons:
- Equipment Cost: Forced carbonation requires additional equipment, such as a CO_2 tank, regulator, and kegging system. This can be an investment if you don't already have these items.
- Oxygen Exposure: Care must be taken to minimize oxygen exposure during the transfer and carbonation process, as excessive oxygen can lead to off-flavors and spoilage.

In Essence:
- Natural Carbonation relies on the yeast to produce CO_2 and is cost-effective and traditional but requires more time and may have inconsistent results.
- Forced Carbonation involves using a CO_2 system to add carbonation directly to the beer, offering precise control and quicker results but requires additional equipment and careful handling.

Both methods can produce excellent beer, and the choice between them depends on your brewing setup, budget, and how quickly you want to enjoy your finished product.

7.3 Storing and Aging Beer

Storing and aging beer is a crucial step in enhancing its flavour, complexity, and overall quality. While not all beers are designed for aging, certain styles benefit greatly from extended storage, allowing the flavors to evolve over time. Proper storage conditions are key to preserving the beer's integrity and achieving the best possible taste.

Why Age Beer?

The aging process in beer can lead to the development of deeper, more complex flavors. Over time, chemical reactions occur between the various components of beer—alcohol, hops, malt, and yeast—which can soften harsh flavors and produce new taste notes. Aging allows the beer to mellow, resulting in smoother textures and more rounded flavors.

Certain beer styles, such as barleywines, imperial stouts, and Belgian ales, are well-suited to aging because of their higher alcohol content and rich malt profiles. These beers typically have stronger flavors and more robust structures, which can improve with time.

Factors That Influence Beer Aging

Several factors impact how a beer ages and whether it improves or degrades during the process:

1. Alcohol Content:

Beers with higher alcohol content (above 7%) tend to age better because alcohol acts as a preservative. Lower alcohol beers, like pale ales or lagers, are generally not suitable for aging as they can lose their freshness and develop off-flavors more quickly.

2. Hop Profile:

Hoppy beers, such as IPAs, are generally not suited for aging because hop aromas and bitterness fade over time, often resulting in a less flavourful beer. These beers are best enjoyed fresh to appreciate their vibrant hop character.

3. Malt Complexity:

Malt-forward beers, such as stouts, porters, and barleywines, tend to age well because the malt sugars and flavors can develop into more complex notes, such as caramel, toffee, chocolate, or dried fruit.

4. Yeast and Bottle Conditioning:

Beers that are bottle-conditioned (i.e., beers that continue to ferment slightly in the bottle due to the presence of yeast) can benefit from aging, as the yeast continues to contribute to flavour evolution over time.

Optimal Storage Conditions for Aging Beer

To successfully age beer, it is essential to store it under the right conditions. Poor storage can lead to undesirable flavors and spoilage.

1. Temperature:

Beer should be stored in a cool, consistent environment. The ideal temperature for aging beer is between 50°F and 60°F (10°C to 15°C). Storing beer at higher temperatures can accelerate chemical reactions, potentially leading to off-flavors, while extremely cold temperatures can stunt the aging process.

2. Darkness:

Light, especially UV light, can quickly spoil beer, leading to a "skunky" taste. Beers should be stored in complete darkness or in opaque bottles to protect them from light exposure. Storing them in a dark cellar or enclosed cabinet is ideal.

3. Humidity:

Maintaining moderate humidity levels (around 50-70%) can help preserve the integrity of the beer's packaging, especially if the beer is sealed with a cork. Low humidity can cause corks to dry out, allowing air to seep in, while high humidity can promote mold growth.

4. Position:

Beers sealed with a cork should be stored on their sides to keep the cork moist and prevent it from drying out. This prevents air from entering the bottle, which could lead to oxidation. Beers with crown caps can be stored upright, which allows sediment to settle at the bottom of the bottle.

The Aging Process: How Flavors Evolve Over Time

As beer ages, several chemical reactions occur that change its flavour profile, aroma, and mouthfeel. These reactions are slow but steady, allowing different flavour compounds to develop and mature.

1. Oxidation:

Over time, a small amount of oxygen will inevitably interact with the beer. In controlled amounts, this oxidation can add subtle flavors, such as sherry, dried fruit, or honey, especially in malt-forward beers. However, excessive oxidation can result in stale or cardboard-like off-flavors, which is why airtight storage is crucial.

2. Malt Flavour Development:

The rich malt flavors in certain beers evolve during aging. Caramel, toffee, and molasses notes may intensify, while harsh or bitter edges soften. Dark beers, like stouts, may develop complex flavors like chocolate, coffee, dried fruit, or even port or wine-like characteristics.

3. Reduction of Bitterness:

Over time, the bitterness from hops diminishes as hop compounds break down. This is why hop-forward beers like IPAs are not ideal for aging, as the vibrant bitterness and floral hop aromas fade, leading to a beer that may taste flat or unbalanced.

4. Carbonation Changes:

Beers with bottle conditioning will continue to develop carbonation as the yeast consumes any residual sugars. Over time, this can lead to a smoother and more refined mouthfeel. However, carbonation may decrease slightly with extended aging if the yeast becomes inactive.

5. Sourness and Funk in Wild Beers:

Beers that use wild yeast strains or bacteria (such as Brettanomyces or Lactobacillus) may develop more pronounced sourness or "funky" flavors as they age. These beers are often intentionally brewed for long-term aging and can develop unique flavors, such as barnyard, leather, or tart fruit.

How Long to Age Beer?

The optimal aging period for beer varies depending on the style and personal preferences. Some beers can age for a few months to improve their balance and complexity, while others may benefit from aging for several years.

- Short-Term Aging (3 to 6 months): Many strong ales, stouts, and porters can benefit from short-term aging to allow flavors to meld and any harsh alcohol notes to mellow out.

- Long-Term Aging (1 to 5 years or more): Stronger beers like barleywines, Belgian quads, and certain imperial stouts may be aged for several years. Over time, these beers develop deep, complex flavors, but they may also reach a peak, after which they can begin to decline in quality.

- Beers That Should Not Be Aged: Lighter beers such as pilsners, wheat beers, pale ales, and most IPAs are best consumed fresh. These beers rely on crispness, hop freshness, and vibrant flavors that fade with time.

Potential Risks of Aging Beer

While aging beer can lead to fantastic results, there are also risks if not done properly:

- Oxidation: If too much oxygen enters the bottle, it can lead to stale, papery flavors.

- Skunking: Exposure to light can cause beer to develop unpleasant "skunky" aromas.

- Loss of Carbonation: If the seal is compromised, the beer may lose its carbonation and become flat.

Storing and aging beer is both an art and a science that allows certain beers to reach their full flavour potential. By providing the right conditions—cool temperatures, darkness, and proper humidity—you can transform a good beer into a great one. However, not all beers benefit from aging, and understanding which styles to age and for how long is key to ensuring the best possible results. With patience and proper care, aged beers can offer a complex, rewarding drinking experience.

CHAPTER 8

RECIPE DEVELOPMENT AND EXPERIMENTATION

8.1 Designing Your Own Beer Recipes

Designing your own beer recipes is one of the most rewarding aspects of brewing. It allows you to get creative, experiment with flavors, and craft a beer that suits your personal preferences. While there's an art to creating something truly unique, the process also involves a good deal of science to ensure the beer ferments properly and has the right balance of flavors. Here's how to approach designing your own beer recipe from start to finish.

1. Start with a Beer Style or Concept

The first step in designing a beer recipe is to decide what kind of beer you want to make. Do you want to stick to traditional beer styles like a pale ale, stout, or lager, or do you want to push boundaries with a unique creation?

- Traditional Styles: If you're aiming for a classic beer, it helps to choose an established style as a foundation. Each beer style has its own guidelines for colour, bitterness, alcohol content, and flavour profile, so knowing what you're aiming for can guide your ingredient choices. Resources like the Beer Judge Certification Program (BJCP) style guidelines are helpful to understand what defines specific styles.

- Creative Concepts: If you're more adventurous, you can start with an idea instead of a specific style. For example, you might want to brew a beer with unique ingredients like coffee, fruit, or spices, or you could aim to create a beer with a particular flavour profile, such as a dessert-like beer with chocolate and vanilla notes.

2. Choose Your Ingredients

Once you've settled on a style or concept, it's time to select the key ingredients that will define your beer: malt, hops, yeast, and water. Each of these ingredients plays a role in the beer's flavour, aroma, and appearance.

i. Malt: The Backbone of Beer

Malt provides the fermentable sugars that yeast converts into alcohol and CO_2 during fermentation, and it also contributes to the beer's colour, sweetness, and body.

- Base Malts: These make up the majority of the grain bill and provide the bulk of the fermentable sugars. Common base malts include pale malt for ales, Pilsner malt for lagers, and Maris Otter for English beers.
- Specialty Malts: Specialty malts add specific flavors and colours to the beer. For example, crystal malt can add caramel sweetness, while roasted malts like chocolate malt or black malt contribute roasted, coffee-like flavors for darker beers like stouts and porters.

When selecting malts, balance is key. Too much specialty malt can make the beer overly sweet, heavy, or unbalanced, so it's important to think about how each malt contributes to the overall flavour profile.

ii. Hops: Bitterness, Flavour, and Aroma

Hops provide bitterness to balance the sweetness of the malt, as well as distinct flavors and aromas depending on the variety used. When designing a recipe, you need to decide how much bitterness you want and what hop flavors to feature.

- Bitterness: Bitterness is measured in International Bitterness Units (IBUs), and each beer style has a typical IBU range. Adding hops early in the boil (60+ minutes) results in more bitterness, while late additions (15-0 minutes) contribute more aroma and flavour but less bitterness.
- Hop Varieties: Hops can impart a wide range of flavors and aromas, from citrus and pine (e.g., Cascade, Simcoe)

to tropical fruit (e.g., Citra, Mosaic) and even earthy or spicy notes (e.g., Saaz, Fuggle). Choose hop varieties based on the style of beer you're brewing and the flavour profile you're aiming for.

iii. Yeast: The Unsung Hero

Yeast is a critical ingredient that not only ferments the beer but also influences its flavour. The two main types of yeast used in brewing are ale yeast (Saccharomyces cerevisiae) and lager yeast (Saccharomyces pastorianus).

- **Ale Yeast:** Ale yeast ferments at warmer temperatures (60-72°F) and tends to produce more fruity and complex flavors, which are characteristic of ales like pale ales, IPAs, and stouts.
- **Lager Yeast:** Lager yeast ferments at cooler temperatures (45-55°F) and produces cleaner, crisper flavors, typical of lagers like pilsners and bocks.

When selecting yeast, consider how it complements the malt and hop flavors. Some yeasts contribute fruity esters or spicy phenols, while others ferment cleanly with little flavour contribution.

iv. Water: The Hidden Ingredient

Water is often overlooked, but it plays a huge role in brewing. The mineral content of your water affects the flavour and mouthfeel of your beer. Brewers typically adjust water chemistry to suit the beer style they're brewing.

- **Hard water** (high in calcium and magnesium) is good for darker beers like stouts and porters.
- **Soft water** (low in minerals) is better for light beers like pilsners and pale ales.

Depending on the style, you may need to adjust the pH of your water and add minerals like calcium sulphate (gypsum) or calcium chloride to achieve the desired flavour and mouthfeel.

3. Formulate Your Recipe

Now that you've selected your ingredients, it's time to put them together in a recipe. A basic beer recipe includes the following elements:

- Grain Bill: The total amount and types of malts you'll use.
- Hop Schedule: When and how much hops to add during the boil (or post-boil for dry hopping).
- Yeast Selection: The strain of yeast and the amount to pitch into the wort.
- Water Adjustments: Any changes to the water chemistry to suit the style.

Here's an example of a simple pale ale recipe:

i. Grain Bill:

- 80% Pale Malt
- 10% Crystal 40L
- 5% Vienna Malt
- 5% Carapils

ii. Hop Schedule:

- 1 oz Cascade (60 min for bitterness)
- 1 oz Cascade (15 min for flavour)
- 1 oz Cascade (0 min for aroma)
- Yeast: American Ale Yeast (Wyeast 1056 or SafAle US-05)
- Water: Adjust for a moderate sulphate to chloride ratio for a balanced hop and malt profile.

4. Calculate Important Metrics

To ensure your recipe results in a balanced beer, it's important to calculate a few key metrics:

- Original Gravity (OG): This measures the amount of sugar in your wort before fermentation and determines the potential alcohol content of your beer. Use brewing software or calculators to estimate the OG based on your grain bill.

- Final Gravity (FG): This measures the remaining sugar after fermentation and indicates the beer's sweetness and body. Yeast selection and fermentation conditions affect the FG.

- Alcohol by Volume (ABV): This is calculated based on the difference between OG and FG. A typical pale ale might have an ABV of 4.5-6%, while stronger beers like barleywines can have ABVs above 10%.

- IBU (International Bitterness Units): This measures the bitterness of your beer. Balance the IBU with the OG to avoid a beer that's too sweet or too bitter. An IPA might have 40-70 IBUs, while a stout might only have 20-40 IBUs.

5. Experiment, Brew, and Refine

Once you have your recipe, it's time to brew! Keep detailed notes during the brewing process, including mash temperatures, fermentation temperatures, and tasting notes during aging. After tasting the final product, think about what worked and what didn't. You can tweak the recipe next time by adjusting the malt bill, hop schedule, or yeast to get closer to your ideal beer.

Designing your own beer recipes is a process that blends creativity with technical precision. By understanding the role of each ingredient and how they interact, you can craft beers that are perfectly tailored to your tastes. Whether you're brewing a classic style or inventing something entirely new, the journey of recipe design adds an exciting layer to the art of brewing.

8.2 Experimenting with Ingredients and Techniques

Experimenting with ingredients and techniques in brewing allows homebrewers to push boundaries, discover new flavors, and develop unique, personalized beer recipes. This creative process encourages brewers to step away from traditional guidelines and explore the endless possibilities of brewing.

Whether you're adding unconventional ingredients or trying advanced brewing techniques, experimentation brings excitement and innovation to the craft.

1. Exploring Unconventional Ingredients

One of the easiest and most fun ways to experiment with brewing is by introducing non-traditional ingredients. From fruits and spices to herbs and even unusual grains, these additions can transform your beer's flavour profile. Here's how to incorporate various unconventional ingredients into your brews:

i. Fruits and Vegetables

Adding fruit or vegetables can give your beer a fresh, seasonal twist. Fruits like cherries, raspberries, oranges, and peaches work well in styles like wheat beers, sours, and Belgian ales. Vegetables like pumpkin or sweet potato are popular in autumn beers.

- When to Add Fruit: Fruits can be added at different stages of brewing, depending on the desired effect. Adding fruit during fermentation gives a fresh, fruity aroma, while adding it in the boil adds a more subdued flavour.

- Quantity and Form: Use fresh, frozen, or even pureed fruit, but be mindful of sugar content as it can affect fermentation. Start with around 1-2 pounds of fruit per gallon of beer and adjust based on your taste.

ii. Spices, Herbs, and Botanicals

Spices and herbs can enhance or completely alter the flavour of your beer, adding complexity and depth. Popular spices include cinnamon, ginger, coriander, and cloves, while herbs like mint, basil, and lavender provide floral or earthy notes.

- When to Add Spices: Spices are typically added toward the end of the boil or during secondary fermentation to preserve their delicate flavors.

- Quantity and Balance: Use spices sparingly to avoid overpowering the beer. A general rule is to start with 1/4 to 1/2 teaspoon of ground spices or 1-2 ounces of whole spices for a 5-gallon batch.

iii. Unusual Grains and Adjuncts

Experimenting with different grains and adjuncts (unmalted ingredients) can alter the beer's body, sweetness, and texture. Oats, rye, spelt, or even ancient grains like quinoa add interesting flavours and textures to the beer.

- Rye: Adds a spicy, slightly dry finish, great for IPAs and rye ales.

- Oats: Increase mouthfeel and provide a creamy texture, often used in stouts.

- Corn and Rice: Common in lighter beers, these adjuncts lighten the body and contribute mild sweetness.

2. Playing with Different Brewing Techniques

Beyond ingredients, adjusting brewing techniques allows brewers to manipulate the brewing process and achieve unique results. Changing methods such as hop addition timing, fermentation techniques, or conditioning can significantly impact the final product.

i. Dry Hopping for Intense Aroma

Dry hopping is the practice of adding hops during or after fermentation, instead of during the boil. This method boosts hop aroma without increasing bitterness, making it a favourite technique for IPAs and pale ales.

- When to Dry Hop: Add hops during the last few days of fermentation or after primary fermentation is complete for maximum aroma.

- How Much to Use: Dry hopping rates vary but can range from 1 to 4 ounces of hops per 5-gallon batch. Experiment with different hop varieties to explore a range of citrusy, floral, or piney aromas.

ii. Cold Steeping for Smoother Flavors

Cold steeping involves soaking specialty grains like roasted malts or coffee beans in cold water rather than hot, minimizing harsh or bitter flavors while still extracting complex notes. This technique is particularly useful when brewing dark beers like porters and stouts.

- Process: Steep the grains in cold water for 12-24 hours, then strain and add the liquid to your wort or secondary fermentation.
- Benefits: Cold steeping leads to smoother, cleaner flavors with less astringency compared to hot steeping.

iii. Brettanomyces and Wild Fermentation

Using wild yeasts like Brettanomyces or incorporating spontaneous fermentation techniques can give your beer funky, tart, or earthy flavors. Wild fermentation is commonly used in sour ales and farmhouse-style beers.

- Brettanomyces (Brett): A wild yeast that produces unique flavors like barnyard, leather, or tropical fruit, depending on how it's used. Brett can ferment sugars that traditional yeasts leave behind, creating complex beers over time.
- Mixed Fermentation: Combine traditional yeast with Brett or bacteria like Lactobacillus and Pediococcus to create sour beers. The balance between sourness and funkiness depends on how these microbes are used.

iv. Barrel Aging for Depth and Complexity

Aging beer in barrels imparts complex flavors like vanilla, oak, or whiskey, depending on the barrel's previous contents. The slow, gradual oxidation and absorption of barrel flavors add depth and complexity to the beer.

- Choosing Barrels: Use whiskey, bourbon, wine, or rum barrels for aging to complement the beer's existing flavour profile.
- How Long to Age: Beers can be aged in barrels for anywhere from a few weeks to several months or even years. Regularly taste the beer to monitor the development of flavors and prevent over-aging.

3. Adjusting Mash and Boil Techniques

Tweaking the mashing and boiling processes can also affect the beer's sweetness, body, and flavour extraction. These adjustments allow you to further customize the outcome of your brew.

i. Step Mashing for Enhanced Fermentability

Step mashing involves gradually increasing the mash temperature in stages to target specific enzyme activity. This allows for more precise control over the beer's body, mouthfeel, and sweetness.

- Beta-Amylase Rest (140-150°F): Produces more fermentable sugars, resulting in a drier beer.
- Alpha-Amylase Rest (158-162°F): Yields less fermentable sugars, creating a fuller, sweeter beer.

ii. Extended Boil for Caramelization

An extended boil can deepen the colour and caramelize the sugars in the wort, leading to richer malt flavors and a darker beer. This is especially useful in beers like barleywines or imperial stouts where bold flavors are desired.

- Boil Times: While most beers are boiled for 60 minutes, extending the boil to 90 or 120 minutes can enhance caramel and toffee-like flavors.

4. Experimenting with Fermentation Conditions

Changing fermentation temperature and conditions can drastically alter the flavour, aroma, and mouthfeel of your beer.

i. Temperature Manipulation

- Low Fermentation Temperatures (50-60°F): Slower fermentation with cleaner, crisper flavors, ideal for lagers or some ales like Kölsch.
- Higher Temperatures (70-80°F): Faster fermentation with more ester and phenol production, resulting in fruity or spicy flavors typical in saisons or Belgian ales.

ii. Secondary Fermentation with Additives

Add fruit, spices, coffee, or other flavouring agents during secondary fermentation for subtle and integrated flavors. This method is gentler than adding ingredients during the boil, helping to preserve delicate flavors and aromas.

5. Monitoring and Adjusting During Experimentation

When experimenting with new ingredients or techniques, it's important to monitor the brewing process closely. Keep detailed notes on ingredient quantities, process adjustments, and how each change impacts the final product.

- Tasting Notes: Take regular taste samples throughout fermentation and aging to evaluate how flavors develop over time.
- Trial and Error: Experimentation is a learning process, so don't be afraid to adjust and retry recipes until you achieve your desired results.

Experimenting with ingredients and techniques in brewing unlocks a world of creativity and innovation. From adding unusual fruits and spices to using advanced fermentation methods, brewers can create unique beers that push the boundaries of traditional styles. By combining creative vision with an understanding of brewing science, homebrewers can craft beers that are not only flavourful and exciting but also entirely their own.

8.3 Scaling Recipes for Larger Batches

Scaling up a brewing recipe for larger batches is a common practice for homebrewers who want to increase their output or transition from homebrewing to commercial production. However, it's not as simple as multiplying ingredients. Several factors need careful adjustment to ensure the beer retains its intended flavour, balance, and quality, even in larger quantities. This process requires attention to ingredient proportions, equipment capacities, and the effects of increased batch size on the brewing process.

1. Adjusting Ingredient Quantities

The most straightforward part of scaling up a recipe is adjusting the amounts of ingredients such as malt, hops, yeast, and water. However, proportional scaling doesn't always apply perfectly to brewing because some ingredients, especially hops and yeast, behave differently in larger volumes.

i. Malt and Grain Bill

The base malt and specialty grains can typically be scaled linearly with batch size. For instance, if you're doubling your batch size from 5 gallons to 10 gallons, you can generally double the amount of grain.

- Considerations for Malt Efficiency: Larger batches may experience slight differences in mash efficiency due to the size of your equipment and heat distribution. It's essential to monitor the efficiency of your larger mash and adjust grain quantities if necessary to maintain your target original gravity (OG).

ii. Hops

Hops are more complex when scaling up. While you can increase the quantity proportionally, hops' bitterness and aroma extraction don't always scale linearly due to factors such as boil time, evaporation rate, and wort volume.

- Bitterness (IBU): Larger boil volumes tend to extract more bitterness from hops, so increasing the amount of hops proportionally may result in an overly bitter beer. You may need to scale hop additions slightly less than 1:1 to achieve the same International Bitterness Units (IBU) as the original recipe.

- Aroma and Flavour Hops: Late-addition and dry-hopped hops for aroma and flavour can often be scaled proportionally without much adjustment, but it's important to taste-test and adjust if the hop character feels too muted or too strong.

iii. Yeast

Scaling yeast for larger batches isn't as simple as increasing the quantity. The number of yeast cells required is proportional to the wort volume and the gravity of the beer, so higher gravity beers will need more yeast, even in the same batch size.

- Pitching Rate: Larger batches often require a higher yeast pitching rate to ensure proper fermentation. Using yeast calculators can help determine the correct number of yeast cells needed for larger volumes, especially when making high-alcohol beers.

- Oxygenation: When brewing larger batches, oxygen levels become critical for yeast health. The larger the batch, the more oxygen is needed during pitching to ensure the yeast can properly ferment.

iv. Water

Water volume increases proportionally with batch size, but water chemistry adjustments may not be linear. The concentration of minerals, pH levels, and the overall water profile should be carefully considered and may require tweaking, especially for larger batches with distinct water needs for certain beer styles.

- Water Chemistry: Larger batches might require different water treatments to achieve the correct balance of ions (like calcium, magnesium, and sulphates). This is especially important when replicating a specific style that relies on precise water profiles, such as a traditional pilsner or stout.

2. Equipment Considerations

Scaling up a recipe requires you to evaluate your equipment's capacity and how it might impact your brewing process. For example, larger volumes may require different approaches to heat management, cooling, and fermentation.

i. Boil Kettle Size and Heat Management

Larger batches require bigger kettles, and with larger volumes, maintaining a consistent boil can become more challenging. Make sure your heating source is powerful enough to bring the wort to a rolling boil without long delays.

- Boil-Off Rate: The boil-off rate might decrease proportionally in larger batches due to a reduced surface area-to-volume ratio, which means less evaporation during the boil. This can affect your final wort concentration and may require adjustments in boil time or kettle size.

ii. Mash Tun Capacity

Scaling up the grain bill means you'll need a larger mash tun with adequate space for increased grain and water. Additionally, the larger volume of grain and water can affect the heat retention and mash consistency.

- Thermal Stability: Maintaining a stable mash temperature becomes more difficult in larger batches. Using insulated or temperature-controlled mash tuns can help ensure consistent conversion of starches to sugars.

iii. Cooling Efficiency

Larger volumes of hot wort take longer to cool down after the boil. Your existing cooling system, such as immersion or counterflow chillers, may not be as efficient at cooling larger batches quickly.

- Cooling Time: Prolonged cooling times can increase the risk of contamination, so you may need to upgrade your chilling system to handle the increased volume effectively.
- Temperature Control: During fermentation, maintaining consistent temperatures becomes even more crucial with larger batches. Larger fermentation vessels may require more robust temperature control systems to ensure proper yeast activity.

3. Adjusting the Brewing Process for Larger Batches

Scaling up a recipe also means considering how the brewing process itself changes with larger quantities. The interaction between ingredients, timing, and environmental factors like heat and oxygen will be more pronounced in larger volumes.

i. Mashing and Lautering

The larger volume of grain and water will affect the mash process. Lautering, or the process of separating wort from the grain, may take longer with larger batches, and more grain means you'll need to carefully manage the sparge to avoid stuck mashes.

- Mash Efficiency: In larger batches, mash efficiency can drop due to the increased volume and heat distribution. Adjusting sparge techniques or increasing the grain slightly can help maintain the desired efficiency.
- Sparging Time: Lautering and sparging times may need to be extended to ensure proper wort collection without causing channelling or inefficiency.

ii. Boil Time and Hop Utilization

In larger boils, the increased volume can lead to slower heat transfer, affecting evaporation and hop utilization. The length of your boil may need to be adjusted to account for a different evaporation rate, which will influence the wort's concentration and bitterness.

- Evaporation Rate: Boil-off rates are typically lower in larger batches, which means the wort won't concentrate as much. Adjust the length of the boil to ensure that you achieve the target gravity.

iii. Fermentation

Larger batches require careful monitoring during fermentation, especially for temperature control and yeast health. Larger volumes generate more heat during active fermentation, which can lead to unintended flavors if not managed.

- Fermentation Vessels: Ensure that your fermenters are large enough to handle the batch size with extra headspace for krausen, the foamy head that forms during active fermentation.
- Temperature Control: Larger fermenters may need more efficient cooling systems to prevent the heat generated by fermentation from rising too high, which could lead to off-flavors.

4. Quality Control in Larger Batches

As the batch size increases, so does the importance of maintaining quality control throughout the process. Consistency is key when scaling up a recipe, especially if you're brewing for commercial purposes.

i. Sampling and Testing

With larger batches, it's crucial to take more frequent samples to monitor gravity, pH, temperature, and flavor throughout the brewing process. This ensures that any adjustments needed to maintain quality are made in time.

- Gravity Checks: Regularly measure the original and final gravities to ensure the beer's strength and sweetness are within the desired range.
- pH Monitoring: Monitor pH levels during mashing, boiling, and fermentation to ensure proper enzyme activity and yeast health.

ii. Sensory Evaluation

Taste-testing at every stage becomes even more important in larger batches. Any small issue in a large batch can lead to significant flavour variations, so early detection of any off-flavors or imbalances can save the batch from being ruined.

- Tasting Notes: Keep detailed records of flavour development, particularly in the fermentation and aging stages, so you can make adjustments in future batches if needed.

Scaling brewing recipes for larger batches requires more than just multiplying ingredient amounts. Careful adjustments to ingredients, equipment, and process management are essential to maintain the beer's flavour, balance, and quality. By paying attention to factors such as hop utilization, yeast pitching, boil-off rates, and fermentation conditions, brewers can successfully scale their recipes while preserving the intended characteristics of the beer.

CHAPTER 9

THE SCIENCE BEHIND FLAVOUR AND AROMA

9.1 Understanding Flavour Profiles in Beer

Flavour profiles in beer are complex and influenced by many factors, including ingredients, brewing techniques, fermentation processes, and maturation. When discussing flavour profiles, it's essential to consider the overall sensory experience a beer provides, which includes taste, aroma, mouthfeel, and aftertaste. Understanding flavour profiles helps brewers craft well-balanced beers and allows beer enthusiasts to appreciate the subtleties in various beer styles.

1. Components of Flavour Profiles

The flavour profile of a beer is shaped by several key components, each contributing distinct characteristics to the overall experience:

i. Malt

Malt is the backbone of any beer and significantly influences its sweetness, body, and flavour complexity. The type of malt used, whether pale, roasted, caramel, or specialty, impacts the flavour in various ways:

- Pale Malt: Contributes to light, bready, or biscuity flavours. Common in lighter beer styles like pilsners or pale ales.

- Caramel or Crystal Malt: Adds sweetness, caramel, toffee, and honey-like flavours, often found in amber ales, porters, and darker beers.

- Roasted Malt: Provides deep, rich flavours such as chocolate, coffee, or burnt toast, commonly found in stouts and porters.

ii. Hops

Hops add bitterness to balance the sweetness of the malt, but they also contribute to a wide range of flavour and aroma characteristics depending on the variety used. Hops are often categorized into two main functions: bitterness hops and aroma/flavour hops.

- Bitterness: Primarily influenced by alpha acids in hops, bitterness is necessary to counteract the sweetness from malt. Strong bitterness is a defining characteristic of styles like IPAs.

- Aroma and Flavour: Hops can contribute fruity, floral, herbal, piney, or citrusy notes depending on the variety. For example:
    - ✓ Citrusy: Hops like Cascade or Citra impart bright, lemon, lime, or grapefruit flavours.
    - ✓ Herbal or Earthy: Hops like Fuggles or Saaz offer more subtle, herbal, and grassy flavours.

iii. Yeast

Yeast not only ferments the sugars in the wort into alcohol but also generates a variety of flavours during fermentation, often referred to as fermentation esters and phenols.

- Esters: Produce fruity flavours, such as banana, pear, or apple, common in ales like Hefeweizens and Belgian beers.

- Phenols: Contribute spicy, clove-like, or peppery flavours, particularly in certain Belgian ales and wheat beers.

- Neutral Yeast Strains: Used in lagers or some ales, these yeast strains contribute minimal flavour, allowing malt and hops to shine.

iv. Water

While often overlooked, water plays a significant role in beer flavour. The mineral content of the brewing water, including calcium, magnesium, and sulphate, affects mouthfeel, bitterness, and malt sweetness. For example:

- Sulphate: Enhances hop bitterness and crispness.

- Chloride: Accentuates malt sweetness and body.

- pH Levels: Can influence the overall balance of flavours.

2. Tasting Components

To fully understand beer flavour profiles, it's essential to break down how the taste components interact. These components include:

i. Sweetness

Derived from the malt, sweetness is the base flavour that provides body and balance to the beer. The level of residual sugar left after fermentation contributes to the perceived sweetness, ranging from dry (minimal sweetness) to sweet (full-bodied).

ii. Bitterness

Bitterness from hops balances the malt's sweetness. It can range from mild and subtle in styles like lagers and brown ales to intense and pronounced in IPAs. The bitterness is measured in International Bitterness Units (IBUs), with higher numbers indicating stronger bitterness.

iii. Sourness

Some beer styles intentionally incorporate sourness, which is primarily the result of lactic acid, acetic acid, or other organic acids produced by wild yeasts or bacteria. Sour beers, such as Berliner Weisse or Lambic, use this characteristic to create tart, refreshing flavours.

iv. Saltiness

Saltiness is rare in beer, but some specialty styles, like Gose, include a touch of salt to enhance the flavour profile. It can add depth and a slight tang to the beer.

v. Umami

Although not as common, umami (savoury flavours) can sometimes be found in certain beers, particularly those with rich, roasted malt, smoked ingredients, or barrel-aged character. These beers may have a meat-like, soy sauce, or mushroom flavour.

3. Aromas in Beer

Aroma is a significant component of a beer's flavour profile, often providing the first impression of what the beer will taste like. The smell is directly related to the ingredients used and the brewing process.

i. Malt Aromas

Depending on the malt type, beer aromas can range from light, sweet notes of honey or biscuits to deeper, richer aromas of caramel, toffee, chocolate, or roasted coffee.

ii. Hop Aromas

Hops contribute a wide variety of aromas, depending on the type and when they are added to the boil. Typical hop aromas include floral, fruity (citrus, berry, tropical), herbal, piney, or earthy notes.

iii. Yeast Aromas

The yeast strain used in brewing can produce distinct aromas. For example:

- Fruity Esters: Bananas, apples, or pears.

- Spicy Phenols: Clove, pepper, or bubble gum-like smells, especially in Belgian-style ales.

4. Mouthfeel and Aftertaste

Mouthfeel refers to the texture of the beer as it's consumed, while aftertaste is the lingering flavour left after swallowing.

i. Mouthfeel

Mouthfeel includes body, carbonation level, and astringency. These factors affect the overall drinking experience:

- Body: Describes the weight or thickness of the beer in the mouth. It can range from light and crisp (e.g., lagers) to heavy and full (e.g., stouts).
- Carbonation: The level of fizz or bubbles can make a beer feel more lively or smooth.
- Astringency: A dry, puckering sensation often caused by tannins from hops or roasted grains, common in IPAs and dark beers.

ii. Aftertaste

The aftertaste can reveal deeper layers of flavour, including eFor instance, a well-hopped IPA may leave a long-lasting bitterness, while a malt-forward stout may finish with a lingering sweetness or roasted character.

5. Flavour Balance

A balanced flavour profile is crucial for a good beer. While one component (such as bitterness or sweetness) may be more prominent in specific styles, a well-made beer will have complementary flavours that don't overpower each other.

i. Malt vs. Hop Balance

In many beers, balance is key. For example, in an IPA, the bitterness from hops should balance the sweetness from malt, preventing the beer from being too bitter or too sweet.

ii. Alcohol Influence

Higher alcohol content can add warming or sweet notes to the beer, but it should be integrated into the overall flavour profile.

Excessive alcohol can result in an overpowering, boozy taste that detracts from the beer's other flavours.

iii. Fermentation Influence

The flavours produced during fermentation, such as esters and phenols, should complement the malt and hop characteristics. For example, in a Belgian Dubbel, fruity esters from yeast work with the caramel malts to create a balanced, complex flavour.

Understanding flavour profiles in beer is about recognizing how ingredients and brewing techniques come together to create a cohesive sensory experience. By paying attention to the interaction between malt sweetness, hop bitterness, yeast-derived flavours, and the role of water, brewers and beer enthusiasts can appreciate the complexity of different beer styles. Through practice, identifying and describing these flavours becomes a rewarding part of the brewing and tasting process.

9.2 The Role of Hops in Aroma and Bitterness

Hops are one of the key ingredients in beer brewing, essential for imparting bitterness, aroma, and flavour. The delicate balance of these characteristics defines a beer's overall taste profile and complexity. Hops come from the Humulus lupulus plant, and their flowers (often referred to as cones) contain compounds that directly affect the brewing process. Understanding the role of hops is critical for achieving the desired beer style and quality.

1. Bitterness: Balancing Sweetness

The primary role of hops in beer is to provide bitterness, which offsets the sweetness from the malt. During the brewing process, the hops are added at different stages, and when they are boiled, their alpha acids are released. These alpha acids undergo a chemical transformation known as isomerization, which creates the bitterness in beer.

- Alpha Acids: The amount of bitterness a hop variety imparts depends on its alpha acid content. The longer hops are boiled, the more alpha acids are converted, increasing the bitterness level. Hops high in alpha acids, such as Chinook or Magnum, are typically used for bittering.

- IBUs (International Bitterness Units): The bitterness of a beer is measured in IBUs, with higher IBUs indicating a more bitter beer. For example, IPAs tend to have high IBUs, while lagers and pilsners are lower.

2. Aroma: Creating Complexity

In addition to bitterness, hops also contribute significantly to the aroma of beer, adding floral, fruity, spicy, or herbal notes. The aroma compounds come from the essential oils present in hops, which are highly volatile and dissipate if boiled for too long. Therefore, hops added late in the brewing process, particularly in the final minutes of boiling or during dry hopping (after fermentation), contribute more to aroma than to bitterness.

- Essential Oils: These oils include myrcene, humulene, caryophyllene, and farnesene. Different hop varieties contain varying levels of these oils, each providing unique aroma characteristics.
    - ✓ Myrcene: Known for fruity, citrus, or piney aromas, dominant in hops like Cascade or Citra.
    - ✓ Humulene: Imparts earthy, woody, or spicy aromas and is prominent in hops such as Saaz and Hallertau.
    - ✓ Caryophyllene and Farnesene: Contribute peppery, floral, or herbal qualities.

3. Flavour: Enhancing the Taste Profile

Beyond aroma and bitterness, hops also enhance the overall flavour profile of beer. The interaction between hops, malt, and yeast creates layers of taste that range from fruity and spicy to earthy and resinous. When brewers experiment with different hop varieties or use techniques like dry hopping, they can craft beers with intricate flavour combinations.

- Hop Flavour Varieties:
    - ✓ Citrusy Hops (like Amarillo or Centennial) add zesty, citrus-forward flavors.

- ✓ Tropical Hops (like Mosaic or Galaxy) contribute notes of mango, pineapple, and passionfruit.
- ✓ Herbal/Spicy Hops (like Saaz or Fuggle) offer more subtle, earthy, and peppery flavors, ideal for traditional European styles.

4. Hop Addition Timing

When hops are added during brewing determines their primary contribution:

- Early Boil (Bittering Hops): Added at the beginning of the boil to extract alpha acids, resulting in more bitterness.
- Mid Boil (Flavour Hops): Added halfway through the boil to contribute both bitterness and flavour.
- Late Boil or Whirlpool (Aroma Hops): Added toward the end of the boil or during the whirlpool stage to enhance aroma without much bitterness.
- Dry Hopping: Hops added post-fermentation contribute mainly to aroma without increasing bitterness, often used for IPAs and other hop-forward beers.

Hops are indispensable in defining the aroma, bitterness, and flavour of beer. Through careful selection of hop varieties and timing of their addition, brewers can create a wide range of beer styles, from the intensely bitter and aromatic IPAs to the more balanced and subtle lagers. Understanding how hops contribute to these elements helps brewers tailor their recipes to achieve the perfect harmony of flavors in their beer.

9.3 How Fermentation Influences Flavour Complexity

Fermentation is a crucial phase in beer production where yeast converts sugars from the malt into alcohol and carbon dioxide. However, beyond this basic conversion, the fermentation process also plays a significant role in developing a beer's complex flavour profile. The interaction between yeast, fermentation conditions, and the ingredients creates a wide range of flavour compounds that define the character of different beer styles.

1. Yeast's Role in Flavor Development

The type of yeast used during fermentation significantly influences the flavour complexity of the beer. Yeast is responsible for producing a variety of compounds that affect taste and aroma. Some of the key flavour compounds generated during fermentation include:

- Esters: These are fruity and floral aroma compounds that develop during fermentation. Different yeasts produce different types of esters. For example:
    - ✓ Ale yeast (Saccharomyces cerevisiae) tends to produce higher levels of esters, contributing fruity flavors like banana, pear, and apple.
    - ✓ Lager yeast (Saccharomyces pastorianus) generally produces fewer esters, resulting in a cleaner, crisper flavour profile.
- Phenols: These are compounds that often add spicy or smoky notes to beer. Certain yeast strains, particularly those used in Belgian or wheat beers, produce phenols that can impart flavors such as clove, pepper, and vanilla.
- Alcohols: In addition to ethanol, which is the primary alcohol in beer, yeast can also produce other alcohols known as fusels. These fusel alcohols contribute to warming sensations and flavors like rose, solvent, or anise.

2. Fermentation Temperature and Flavor Complexity

The temperature at which fermentation occurs has a dramatic impact on the flavors produced by yeast. Different yeast strains behave differently at various temperatures:

- Warm Fermentation (18–24°C / 64–75°F): Common with ale yeast, higher temperatures encourage the production of esters and phenols, leading to more complex, fruity, and spicy flavors.
- Cool Fermentation (7–13°C / 45–55°F): Used primarily for lagers, cooler temperatures result in fewer esters and phenols, creating a cleaner, crisper beer with subtle malt and hop flavors dominating.

Controlling the fermentation temperature allows brewers to fine-tune the flavour balance in their beer. Too high a temperature can lead to the production of unwanted off-flavors, such as fusel alcohols or excessive ester production.

3. Oxygen Levels and Yeast Health

Oxygen management during fermentation is crucial for yeast performance and flavour development. While yeast requires oxygen during the initial phase to multiply, excessive oxygen during fermentation can lead to oxidation, which creates undesirable flavors such as cardboard or stale notes.

- Oxygen in Early Fermentation: A small amount of oxygen at the start of fermentation ensures healthy yeast growth, which is important for a clean and controlled fermentation process.
- Oxygen in Later Stages: Introducing oxygen after fermentation can lead to off-flavors, particularly in hop-forward beers, where oxidation can cause a dulling of hop aroma and bitterness.

4. Secondary Fermentation and Aging

During secondary fermentation, additional flavors continue to develop as the yeast processes any remaining sugars and compounds in the beer. For example, certain styles like Belgian ales or wild-fermented beers benefit from extended aging or secondary fermentation, which can produce deeper, more complex flavors.

- Bottle Conditioning: In some cases, brewers add sugar and yeast to bottles to continue fermentation after bottling. This can create a more complex flavour as the beer matures in the bottle, adding depth and carbonation.
- Barrel Aging: In beers aged in barrels, secondary fermentation can introduce new flavors from the wood, as well as from any bacteria or wild yeast present in the barrel. This is common in sour beers or barrel-aged stouts, where flavors like vanilla, oak, and tart fruit emerge.

5. Influence of Wild Yeasts and Bacteria

Wild yeasts (like Brettanomyces) and bacteria (like Lactobacillus or Pediococcus) can also contribute to flavour complexity during fermentation. These organisms produce flavors that are distinct from traditional brewer's yeast, such as:

- Sourness: Lactic acid bacteria produce a tart, sour flavour that is characteristic of beers like Berliner Weisse or Gose.

- Funkiness: Brettanomyces adds earthy, funky, or even barnyard-like flavors, which are prized in beers like Lambics or farmhouse ales.

Fermentation is far more than just the process of converting sugars into alcohol; it is a dynamic phase where yeast, temperature, oxygen levels, and the presence of additional microorganisms all interact to create a wide array of flavors. By understanding and controlling these factors, brewers can craft beers with diverse and intricate flavour profiles that range from fruity and spicy to clean and crisp, with endless possibilities for complexity and depth.

CHAPTER 10

ADVANCED FERMENTATION TECHNIQUES

10.1 High Gravity Brewing and Fermentation

High gravity brewing involves creating beers with a higher original gravity, which means they start with a higher concentration of sugars and fermentable materials. This can lead to stronger, more robust beers with higher alcohol content. Here's a straightforward guide to understanding high gravity brewing and how it affects fermentation:

1. What is High Gravity Brewing?

High gravity brewing refers to the process of brewing beer with a higher-than-normal concentration of sugars before fermentation. This typically means the wort (the liquid extracted from malted grains) has a higher specific gravity or density. High gravity brewing is often used to make strong ales, barleywines, and other high-alcohol beers.

2. Challenges of High Gravity Brewing:

- Yeast Stress: Yeast can become stressed when fermenting high gravity wort due to the higher alcohol levels and increased sugar concentration. This stress can lead to incomplete fermentation or off-flavors.

- Fermentation Issues: High gravity worts can have higher osmotic pressure, which makes it harder for yeast to ferment the sugars. This can lead to a stuck fermentation if not managed properly.

- Flavor Balance: Stronger beers can have intense flavors, which might need careful balancing to ensure the final beer is enjoyable. High gravity brewing often requires more attention to flavour development and ingredient balance.

3. Managing High Gravity Brewing:

- Yeast Selection: Choose a yeast strain that is known for its ability to handle high gravity conditions. Some yeast strains are better suited for high alcohol levels and high sugar concentrations.

- Oxygenation: Properly oxygenate the wort before pitching yeast. This helps the yeast grow and reproduce effectively, which is crucial for handling high gravity worts.

- Gradual Fermentation: Consider starting fermentation at a lower temperature and gradually increasing it as the yeast becomes acclimated. This can help reduce yeast stress and improve fermentation efficiency.

- Nutrient Addition: Add yeast nutrients to support healthy yeast activity. High gravity worts can be deficient in essential nutrients, so adding a nutrient blend can help prevent fermentation problems.

- Fermentation Temperature Control: Maintain a consistent fermentation temperature to avoid stressing the yeast. Extreme temperature fluctuations can lead to off-flavours and fermentation issues.

4. Post-Fermentation Considerations:

    - Conditioning Time: High gravity beers often benefit from extended conditioning periods. Allow the beer to age and mature to develop its flavors and smooth out any harshness.
    - Dilution (Optional): If the beer is too strong or the fermentation was incomplete, you might consider diluting the beer with water or additional wort to achieve the desired balance and alcohol content.

5. Best Practices for High Gravity Brewing:

    - Planning: Plan your brewing process carefully, considering the impact of high gravity on yeast health and fermentation. Prepare for additional steps and adjustments needed for high gravity brewing.
    - Monitoring: Regularly monitor the fermentation progress and gravity levels. This helps ensure that fermentation is proceeding as expected and allows for timely interventions if issues arise.

High gravity brewing involves creating stronger beers with higher sugar concentrations, which can pose challenges for fermentation and flavour balance. By selecting the right yeast, properly oxygenating the wort, and managing fermentation conditions, you can successfully brew high gravity beers and achieve the desired results.

10.2 Barrel Aging and Secondary Fermentation

Barrel aging and secondary fermentation are techniques used to enhance the complexity and character of beer. Here's a simple guide to understanding these processes and how they can improve your brew:

1. What is Barrel Aging?

Barrel aging involves transferring beer into wooden barrels to age for a period of time. This process can impart additional flavors and aromas from the wood and any previous contents of the barrel (like whiskey, wine, or other spirits). It's commonly used for creating complex and flavourful beers such as stouts, porters, and sour ales.

2. Benefits of Barrel Aging:

- Flavor Development: The wood of the barrel can add flavors such as vanilla, oak, or spice to the beer. If the barrel previously held spirits or wine, it can contribute additional notes from those beverages.

- Complexity: Aging in a barrel can develop more nuanced and complex flavors over time, making the beer richer and more layered.

- Smoothing: Barrel aging can help mellow and smooth out harsh flavors, giving the beer a more refined character.

3. What is Secondary Fermentation?

Secondary fermentation occurs after the primary fermentation is complete. During this phase, the beer is transferred from the primary fermenter to a secondary vessel (often a carboy or barrel). This process allows the beer to continue fermenting and maturing, often leading to improved clarity and flavour stability.

4. Benefits of Secondary Fermentation:

- Flavour Maturation: Secondary fermentation allows flavors to meld and mature, leading to a more balanced and harmonious beer.

- Clarity: This stage helps in the settling of yeast and sediment, resulting in a clearer beer.

- Additional Flavouring: It's an opportunity to add extra ingredients like fruit, spices, or herbs to enhance the beer's flavour profile.

5. How to Barrel Age and Perform Secondary Fermentation:

- Barrel Preparation: Before using a barrel, it's important to clean and sanitize it thoroughly. If the barrel is new or hasn't been used recently, you may need to rinse it several times to remove any residual compounds.

- Transfer Process: Carefully transfer your beer from the primary fermenter to the barrel or secondary vessel. Avoid splashing or introducing oxygen, which can cause oxidation and off-flavors.

- Aging Time: The aging time can vary depending on the beer style and desired outcome. It can range from a few weeks to several months. Regularly taste the beer to monitor its development.

- Monitoring: Keep an eye on the aging process. Make sure the barrel or secondary vessel is sealed properly to prevent contamination. Check for any signs of off-flavors or spoilage.

- Packaging: Once aging is complete, carefully transfer the beer to bottles or kegs. Be gentle to avoid disturbing any sediment that may have settled during aging.

Tips for Successful Barrel Aging and Secondary Fermentation:

i. Plan Ahead: Allow sufficient time for aging and secondary fermentation. Rushing these processes can result in a less developed flavour profile.

ii. Sanitize Thoroughly: Proper sanitation is crucial to prevent contamination. Clean and sanitize all equipment and barrels before use.

iii. Taste Regularly: Periodically taste the beer during aging to ensure it's developing as expected. This helps you decide when it's ready for bottling.

Barrel aging and secondary fermentation are methods used to enhance beer's flavors and complexity. Barrel aging adds unique wood and spirit notes, while secondary fermentation improves clarity and allows for flavour maturation. By carefully managing these processes, you can create a more refined and flavourful beer.

10.3 Using Wild Yeasts and Bacteria for Unique Flavors

Using wild yeasts and bacteria in brewing can add distinctive and complex flavors to your beer that you can't achieve with traditional brewing yeasts alone. Here's a clear guide to understanding how these microorganisms can transform your brew:

1. What are Wild Yeasts and Bacteria?

- Wild Yeasts: These are yeast strains that occur naturally in the environment, such as on fruit skins, in the air, or on brewing equipment. Examples include Brettanomyces, which can produce unique flavors like funkiness or earthiness.

- Wild Bacteria: These microorganisms, like Lactobacillus and Pediococcus, can introduce sourness and complexity to your beer. They are commonly used in sour and wild ales.

2. Benefits of Using Wild Yeasts and Bacteria:

- Complex Flavors: Wild yeasts and bacteria can create a wide range of flavors, from fruity and spicy to sour and funky. This can add depth and uniqueness to your beer.

- Diverse Styles: They are often used in brewing styles like lambics, gueuze, and Berliner Weisse, which are known for their complex flavour profiles.

- Creative Freedom: Using wild yeasts and bacteria allows you to experiment with unconventional flavors and create one-of-a-kind beers.

3. How to Use Wild Yeasts and Bacteria:

- Selection: Choose appropriate wild yeasts and bacteria strains based on the flavour profile you want to achieve. You can use commercial blends or harvest them from natural sources like fruit or spontaneously fermented beers.

- Inoculation: Introduce wild yeasts and bacteria into your wort during fermentation. This can be done by adding a small amount of a starter culture or by using a technique called "spontaneous fermentation," where the wort is

- exposed to the environment to capture wild microorganisms.

- Fermentation Conditions: Wild yeasts and bacteria often require different fermentation conditions compared to traditional yeasts. They may need higher temperatures or extended fermentation times to develop their full flavour potential.

- Blending: Sometimes, brewers will blend beers fermented with wild yeasts and bacteria with other batches to achieve a balanced flavour. This technique is often used to create complex, multi-dimensional beers.

4. Managing Wild Fermentation:

- Sanitation: Wild yeasts and bacteria can be unpredictable and may cause contamination if not managed carefully. Ensure all equipment is thoroughly cleaned and sanitized to avoid cross-contamination with other batches.

- Monitoring: Keep an eye on the fermentation process. Wild yeasts and bacteria can produce unexpected flavors, so regular tasting helps ensure the beer develops as desired.

- Patience: Wild fermentation can take longer than standard fermentation. Be prepared for a longer aging process, and allow time for flavors to mature and meld.

Tips for Successful Wild Yeast and Bacteria Brewing:

- Research: Study different wild yeast and bacteria strains to understand their flavour profiles and fermentation requirements. This helps in selecting the right microorganisms for your desired outcome.

- Experiment: Don't be afraid to experiment with small batches. This allows you to test different strains and techniques without risking a large amount of beer.

- Record Keeping: Keep detailed notes on your brewing process, including the strains used, fermentation conditions, and tasting results. This helps you refine your techniques and replicate successful brews.

Using wild yeasts and bacteria in brewing can create unique and complex flavors, offering a creative way to enhance your beer. By carefully selecting strains, managing fermentation conditions, and monitoring the process, you can develop distinctive beers with a rich variety of flavours.

CHAPTER 11

TROUBLESHOOTING COMMON FERMENTATION ISSUES

11.1 Identifying Off-Flavours and Their Causes

Off-flavours in beer are undesirable tastes or aromas that can affect the quality of your brew. Recognizing and understanding these off-flavours is key to improving your brewing process. Here's a simple guide to help you identify common off-flavours and their causes:

1. Common Off-Flavours and Their Causes:

- Skunky (Light struck): This off-flavour often smells like a skunk and is caused by exposure to light. Light can react with compounds in the beer, especially if it's stored in clear or green bottles. To prevent this, store your beer in a dark place or use amber bottles that protect against light.

- Oxidized (Cardboard or Sherry-like): An oxidized beer might taste stale, like cardboard or sherry. This is usually due to excessive oxygen exposure during brewing or bottling. To avoid this, manage oxygen levels carefully and ensure all equipment is well-sealed.

- Buttery (Diacetyl): A buttery or slick taste is often caused by diacetyl, a by product of yeast that didn't fully ferment or clean up. This can happen if fermentation is too warm or if the beer is not given enough time to condition. Ensure proper fermentation temperatures and allow enough time for the yeast to clean up diacetyl.

- Sour (Acidic or Vinegar-like): A sour taste can indicate the presence of wild yeast or bacteria, which can produce acids. This might occur from poor sanitation or unintended microbial contamination. Maintain strict sanitation practices to avoid this issue.

- Metallic: A metallic taste is usually due to contact with metal, such as from metal equipment or containers. Make sure all equipment is made from food-safe materials and thoroughly cleaned.

- Phenolic (Medicinal or Band-Aid-like): Phenolic off-flavours can taste medicinal or like a Band-Aid and are often caused by high fermentation temperatures or the use of certain yeast strains. Ferment at the recommended temperatures for your yeast and ensure proper yeast selection and handling.

- Yeasty (Bready or Doughy): A yeasty flavour can occur if the beer is not properly fermented or if yeast is not fully removed before bottling. This can be managed by ensuring a complete fermentation and proper sediment removal.

2. How to Identify Off-Flavours:

- Taste Testing: Regularly taste your beer at different stages to detect any off-flavours early. Compare your beer to style guidelines to understand what is expected.

- Smell Analysis: Off-flavours often have distinct smells. Use your nose to detect any unusual aromas that could indicate problems.

- Consult Resources: Use brewing guides, forums, and experts to help identify and understand off-flavours.

3. Preventing Off-Flavours:

- Sanitation: Maintain excellent cleanliness and sanitation practices to prevent contamination.

- Temperature Control: Manage fermentation temperatures carefully to avoid producing unwanted by products.

- Proper Handling: Avoid exposing beer to light or oxygen during brewing, fermentation, and packaging.

- Equipment Quality: Use high-quality, food-safe equipment to avoid metallic or other unwanted flavors.

Identifying off-flavours involves recognizing undesirable tastes and understanding their causes. By following good brewing practices, including proper sanitation, temperature control, and equipment handling, you can prevent and address these issues to produce better-tasting beer.

11.2 Dealing with Stuck Fermentations

A stuck fermentation occurs when the yeast stops working before the fermentation process is complete, leaving your beer with higher-than-desired residual sugars and a potentially incomplete flavour profile. Here's a straightforward guide to understanding and dealing with stuck fermentations:

1. What is a Stuck Fermentation?

A stuck fermentation is when yeast activity halts prematurely, and the beer fails to reach the expected final gravity. This results in a sweeter, less fermented beer and can sometimes lead to off-flavors or clarity issues.

2. Common Causes of Stuck Fermentations:

- Temperature Issues: Yeast activity can slow down or stop if the fermentation temperature is too high or too low. Each yeast strain has an ideal temperature range, and deviations can affect fermentation.

- Nutrient Deficiency: Yeast requires certain nutrients to thrive. A lack of essential nutrients can cause yeast to become inactive. This often happens if the wort is deficient in nutrients or if yeast is pitched at too high a concentration without proper aeration.

- High Alcohol Content: If the alcohol content of the beer gets too high, it can inhibit yeast activity. This can be due to high original gravity or excessive sugar content in the wort.

- Yeast Health: Old or improperly stored yeast may not be effective. Using yeast that is past its prime can result in sluggish or incomplete fermentation.

- Oxygen Levels: Insufficient oxygen in the wort before fermentation can lead to a stuck fermentation. Yeast needs oxygen to multiply and begin fermentation effectively.

3. How to Diagnose a Stuck Fermentation:

- Check the Gravity: Use a hydrometer or refractometer to measure the specific gravity of your beer. If the gravity hasn't changed over several days, fermentation may be stuck.

- Inspect the Temperature: Verify that the fermentation temperature is within the recommended range for your yeast strain.

- Evaluate Yeast Health: Consider whether you used fresh, properly stored yeast and whether it was properly rehydrated or pitched.

4. How to Fix a Stuck Fermentation:

- Adjust Temperature: If the temperature is too high or too low, adjust it to the optimal range for your yeast. Sometimes gently warming the fermenter can help restart yeast activity.

- Aerate the Wort: If oxygen levels are low, gently stir or shake the fermenter to reintroduce oxygen. Be cautious to avoid contamination.

- Add Yeast Nutrients: If you suspect a nutrient deficiency, add yeast nutrients or energizers to provide the yeast with what it needs to complete fermentation.

- Pitch More Yeast: If the original yeast is no longer viable, consider pitching a fresh batch of yeast. Ensure that it is the same or a compatible strain for best results.

- Check for Contamination: If you suspect contamination, ensure that all equipment and the fermenter are clean and sanitized. In some cases, you may need to restart fermentation with new yeast.

Prevention Tips:

i. Maintain Proper Sanitation: Ensure all equipment is thoroughly cleaned and sanitized to avoid contamination.

ii. Monitor Fermentation Conditions: Keep track of fermentation temperatures and nutrient levels throughout the process.

iii. Use Fresh Yeast: Always use fresh, properly stored yeast and follow the manufacturer's recommendations for rehydration or pitching.

A stuck fermentation can result from temperature issues, nutrient deficiencies, high alcohol content, poor yeast health, or low oxygen levels. To address it, check the gravity, adjust the temperature, add yeast nutrients, and consider pitching additional yeast if needed. Proper sanitation and monitoring will help prevent stuck fermentations and ensure successful brewing.

11.3 Preventing and Addressing Contamination

Contamination in brewing refers to the presence of unwanted microorganisms that can spoil your beer, causing off-flavours, aromas, and potentially ruining your batch. Here's a simple guide to preventing and addressing contamination in your brewing process:

1. Understanding Contamination:

Contamination can occur when unwanted bacteria, wild yeast, or mold get into your beer. These microorganisms can compete with your brewing yeast, leading to unpleasant flavors, sourness, or even spoilage.

2. Preventing Contamination:

- Sanitation: This is the most critical step in preventing contamination. All equipment, including fermenters, bottles, and utensils, should be thoroughly cleaned and sanitized. Use a food-safe sanitizer, and follow the manufacturer's instructions to ensure that all surfaces are properly treated.

- Proper Cleaning: Before sanitizing, clean your equipment to remove any leftover residues or debris. Use hot water and a suitable cleaner to scrub away any organic matter.

- Handling: Minimize direct contact with your beer or wort to reduce the risk of introducing contaminants. Always use clean tools and avoid touching the inside of bottles or fermenters.

- Air Quality: Keep your brewing area clean and free of dust or mold. Cover your fermenters with a sanitized lid or airlock to prevent airborne contaminants from entering.

- Yeast Management: Use fresh, high-quality yeast and store it properly. Follow the instructions for rehydrating or pitching yeast to ensure it's healthy and ready for fermentation.

3. Identifying Contamination:

- Visual Signs: Look for unusual cloudiness, sediment, or mold growth in your beer. These can be indicators of contamination.

- Smell: Contaminated beer may have off-smells such as sourness, barnyard-like aromas, or other unpleasant odours.

- Taste: Contaminated beer might taste sour, funky, or otherwise different from what you expected.

4. Addressing Contamination:

- Isolate the Problem: If you notice contamination, isolate the affected batch to prevent it from spreading to other batches or equipment.

- Evaluate and Clean: Re-examine your sanitation and handling practices to identify any potential sources of contamination. Clean and sanitize all equipment thoroughly before starting a new batch.

- Dispose of Affected Beer: If contamination is severe and cannot be corrected, it's best to dispose of the affected beer. It's important to avoid drinking or serving contaminated beer as it can be unsafe.

- Seek Advice: If you're unsure about the source of contamination or how to handle it, consult with experienced brewers or brewing resources for guidance.

5. Best Practices for Future Brewing:

- Regular Sanitation: Make sanitation a regular part of your brewing routine. Consistent cleaning and sanitizing will help prevent contamination and improve your brewing results.

- Monitor Conditions: Keep a clean brewing environment and monitor all conditions, including fermentation temperatures and ingredient storage.

- Keep Records: Maintain detailed records of your brewing process to help identify any potential issues and improve your brewing practices over time.

To end with, preventing contamination involves thorough cleaning and sanitizing, proper handling of ingredients, and maintaining a clean brewing environment. Identifying contamination early and addressing it promptly will help ensure that your beer remains high-quality and free from undesirable flavors or spoilage.

CONCLUSION

Beer is a complex and multifaceted beverage with a rich history, diverse flavors, and a variety of brewing techniques. Understanding how beer is made and how different factors influence its flavour can greatly enhance your appreciation and enjoyment of this craft.

Takeaways:

- Fermentation Fundamentals: Fermentation is a crucial process in beer production, where yeast converts sugars into alcohol and produces a range of flavour compounds. The type of yeast, fermentation temperature, and duration all play significant roles in shaping the final taste of the beer.
- Brewing Process: From malting and mashing to fermentation and aging, each step in the brewing process contributes to the beer's overall profile. Mastery of these processes allows brewers to craft a wide range of beer styles with unique characteristics.
- Flavor Evaluation: Properly tasting and evaluating beer involves examining its appearance, aroma, flavour, and mouthfeel. Recognizing common flavour descriptors and

their sources helps in understanding and appreciating the complexity of different beers.
- Experimentation and Creativity: Brewing is both an art and a science. Designing your own recipes, experimenting with ingredients, and scaling recipes for larger batches can lead to exciting new flavors and beer styles.

- Continuous Learning: The world of beer is vast and ever-evolving. Whether you're a homebrewer, a craft beer enthusiast, or simply curious, there's always more to learn and discover. Tasting a variety of beers, exploring different styles, and staying informed about brewing techniques can enhance your knowledge and enjoyment of beer.

By following these principles and continuing to explore the world of beer, you can deepen your understanding of this fascinating beverage and develop a refined palate that appreciates the artistry and science behind every brew. Cheers to your journey in the world of beer

APPENDIX

Glossary of Brewing and Fermentation Terms

Understanding the terminology used in brewing and fermentation can help you navigate the world of beer production more effectively. Here's a glossary of key terms to get you started:

A

- ABV (Alcohol By Volume): A measurement of the alcohol content in a beverage, expressed as a percentage of the total volume.
- Adjuncts: Ingredients added to the brewing process other than the four primary ingredients (water, malt, hops, yeast), such as fruits, spices, or sugars.

B

- Bittering Hops: Hops added early in the brewing process to contribute bitterness and balance the sweetness of the malt.
- Brewing: The process of making beer, involving mashing, boiling, fermenting, conditioning, and packaging.

C

- Carbonation: The presence of dissolved carbon dioxide in beer, which gives it its fizzy quality. It can be natural (from fermentation) or forced (added after brewing).
- Conditioning: The process of allowing beer to mature after fermentation, which can improve flavour and clarity.

D

- Draft Beer: Beer served directly from a keg rather than from a bottle or can.
- Diacetyl: A compound that can impart a buttery flavour to beer, often considered a flaw. It is typically removed during fermentation or conditioning.

E

- Extract: A concentrated form of malt used in brewing, often as a substitute for all-grain brewing. It comes in liquid or dry form.
- Efficiency: A measure of how effectively the mash process converts starches into sugars.

F

- Fermentation: The process by which yeast converts sugars into alcohol and carbon dioxide, producing beer.
- Final Gravity (FG): The specific gravity of beer once fermentation is complete, indicating the final alcohol content and residual sugar levels.

G

- Gravity: A measurement of the density of the liquid compared to water. It helps estimate the amount of sugar available for fermentation.
- Gushing: The uncontrolled overflow of beer from a bottle or can when opened, often due to excessive carbonation or contamination.

H

- Hop Varieties: Different types of hops used in brewing, each contributing unique flavors and aromas. Examples include Cascade, Saaz, and Centennial.
- Hop Bitterness: The level of bitterness contributed by hops to balance the sweetness of the malt.

I

- IBU (International Bitterness Units): A scale used to measure the bitterness of beer, determined by the concentration of iso-alpha acids from hops.
- Infection: Unwanted microorganisms contaminating the beer, leading to off-flavors or spoilage.

L

- Lautering: The process of separating the wort (unfermented beer) from the solid grain husks after mashing.
- Lager: A type of beer brewed using bottom-fermenting yeast at cooler temperatures, resulting in a clean, crisp flavour.

M

- Mashing: The process of mixing crushed malt with hot water to convert starches into fermentable sugars.
- Malt: Germinated cereal grains, usually barley, that are dried and used as a primary ingredient in brewing to provide fermentable sugars and flavour.

N

- Nitrates: Compounds that can affect the flavour and quality of beer if present in high levels, often originating from water sources or ingredients.

O

- Original Gravity (OG): The specific gravity of the wort before fermentation begins, used to estimate the potential alcohol content of the beer.
- Oxygenation: The process of adding oxygen to the wort or beer to aid yeast growth during fermentation, but excessive oxygen can lead to spoilage.

P

- Priming Sugar: Sugar added to beer before bottling to create carbonation through secondary fermentation in the bottle.
- Pilsner: A pale lager with a crisp, clean taste and a noticeable hop bitterness.

R

- Remnant: Any leftover beer or ingredients from a batch that might be used in future brewing or discarded.
- Racking: The process of transferring beer from one vessel to another, typically to separate it from sediment or to prepare it for conditioning.

S

- Secondary Fermentation: The stage after primary fermentation where beer is conditioned and flavors mature, often in a different vessel.
- Souring: The process of intentionally introducing wild yeast or bacteria to create a tart, acidic flavour in beer.

T

- Trub: The sediment of hops, yeast, and proteins that settles at the bottom of the fermenter after fermentation.
- Taste: The sensory experience of flavors and aromas detected through the mouth and nose, crucial for evaluating beer.

W

- Wort: The liquid extracted from malted grains during mashing, which is then boiled and fermented to produce beer.
- Wyeast: A brand of yeast used in brewing, known for its various strains and high-quality products.

Yeast

- Yeast Strains: Different types of yeast used in brewing, such as ale yeast (top-fermenting) and lager yeast (bottom-fermenting), each contributing unique characteristics to the beer.

Z

- Zymurgy: The study or practice of fermentation in brewing, winemaking, and distilling.

This glossary covers essential terms related to brewing and fermentation, helping you better understand the processes and concepts involved in creating and enjoying beer.

PROJECTS

1. Ale Brewing Process

Ales are fermented with top-fermenting yeast at warmer temperatures, which typically results in a shorter fermentation time and a more complex, fruity, and robust flavour.

Step-by-Step Process for Brewing an Ale:

1. Choose Ingredients:

- Malt: Pale malts such as Maris Otter or Pilsner malt are common for ales.
- Hops: Select aromatic hops like Cascade, Centennial, or Fuggle for bitterness and aroma.

- Yeast: Use a top-fermenting yeast strain, such as Saccharomyces cerevisiae.
- Water: Use filtered water with moderate mineral content.

2. Malting and Mashing:
   - Crush your malt to expose the starches.
   - Heat water in your mash tun to around 150-158°F (65-70°C).
   - Add crushed malt to water and hold the temperature for about 60 minutes to convert starches to fermentable sugars.

3. Lautering:
   - Separate the liquid wort from the grain by sparging (rinsing the grains with hot water) to collect more sugars.

4. Boiling and Hop Addition:
   - Bring the wort to a rolling boil for 60-90 minutes.
   - Add hops at the beginning of the boil for bitterness, in the middle for flavour, and near the end for aroma.

5. Cooling the Wort:
   - Use a wort chiller or ice bath to cool the wort to around 65-72°F (18-22°C).

6. Fermentation:
   - Transfer the cooled wort to a sanitized fermentation vessel.
   - Pitch the yeast and maintain the fermentation temperature at 65-72°F (18-22°C).
   - Primary fermentation lasts about 1-2 weeks.

7. Conditioning and Bottling:
   - Allow the beer to condition for another week in the fermenter or bottle with priming sugar for carbonation.

8. Aging:

- Ales can be aged for a couple of weeks at room temperature for the best flavour development.

2. Lager Brewing Process

Lagers are fermented with bottom-fermenting yeast at cooler temperatures, resulting in a cleaner, crisper flavour. The fermentation process takes longer than that of ales.

Step-by-Step Process for Brewing a Lager:

1. Choose Ingredients:

- Malt: Pilsner malt or 2-row malt is typically used.
- Hops: Noble hops like Saaz, Hallertau, or Tettnanger.
- Yeast: Use a bottom-fermenting lager yeast strain like Saccharomyces pastorianus.
- Water: Soft water with low mineral content works best for lagers.

2. Malting and Mashing:

- Mash at a slightly lower temperature than ales (145-150°F or 63-65°C) to create a more fermentable wort, which results in a drier beer.
- Hold the mash for 60-90 minutes.

3. Lautering:

- Sparge to collect as much fermentable sugar as possible.

4. Boiling and Hop Addition:

- Boil the wort for 60-90 minutes.
- Add hops early for bitterness and sparingly at the end for a clean taste.

5. Cooling the Wort:

- Cool the wort to a much lower temperature, around 45-55°F (7-13°C).

6. Fermentation:
   - Transfer the cooled wort to a sanitized fermenter and pitch your lager yeast.
   - Ferment at 45-55°F (7-13°C) for 2-3 weeks.

7. Lagering (Cold Conditioning):
   - After fermentation, transfer the beer to a secondary fermenter or keg and store at 35-40°F (1-4°C) for 4-6 weeks for smoothness and clarity.

8. Carbonation and Bottling:
   - Bottle with priming sugar or keg and carbonate. Lagers benefit from longer aging.

3. Sour Brewing Process

Sours are brewed by intentionally introducing wild yeasts or bacteria to create tart, acidic flavors.

Step-by-Step Process for Brewing a Sour:

1. Choose Ingredients
   - Malt: A pale base malt like Pilsner or wheat malt is common.
   - Hops: Low bitterness is desired, so use small amounts of noble hops.
   - Yeast and Bacteria: Use traditional ale yeast (Saccharomyces cerevisiae), and add wild yeast (Brettanomyces) or bacteria (Lactobacillus, Pediococcus) for souring.
   - Water: Soft water works best.

2. Malting and Mashing:
   - Mash as usual at 150°F (65°C) for 60 minutes.

3. Lautering:
- Sparge and collect your wort for boiling.

4. Boiling and Hop Addition:
- Boil the wort for 60 minutes, but add only minimal hops to keep the bitterness low.

5. Cooling the Wort:
- Cool to 65-72°F (18-22°C).

6. Fermentation and Souring:
- Pitch the primary yeast for standard fermentation.
- After primary fermentation, introduce wild yeast or bacteria into the secondary fermentation vessel.
- Allow souring for anywhere from several weeks to several months, depending on the desired level of acidity.

7. Aging:
- Sour beers benefit from extended aging, sometimes up to a year, to allow the flavors to develop fully.

8. Bottling:
- Bottle with priming sugar or keg for carbonation.

4. Stout Brewing Process

Stouts are rich, dark ales that typically use roasted barley and malts to achieve their characteristic flavors.

Step-by-Step Process for Brewing a Stout:

1. Choose Ingredients:
- Malt: Use roasted barley, chocolate malt, and black patent malt for a deep colour and flavour.

- Hops: Choose hops with moderate bitterness, such as East Kent Goldings or Fuggle.
- Yeast: Use a top-fermenting yeast, such as English or Irish ale yeast.
- Water: Medium to hard water with higher carbonate levels is ideal.

2. Malting and Mashing:
   - Mash at 152-156°F (67-69°C) for a full-bodied stout.
   - Hold the mash for 60 minutes.

3. Lautering:
   - Sparge and collect wort, ensuring good extraction from the dark malts.

4. Boiling and Hop Addition:
   - Boil for 60 minutes.
   - Add hops early for bitterness to balance the malty sweetness.

5. Cooling the Wort:
   - Cool to 65-72°F (18-22°C).

6. Fermentation:
   - Pitch your yeast and ferment at ale temperatures (65-72°F or 18-22°C) for 1-2 weeks.

7. Conditioning:
   - Stouts benefit from aging. Allow the stout to condition in the fermenter or bottles for at least 4 weeks.

8. Carbonation and Bottling:
   - Stouts are typically low to moderately carbonated. Bottle with priming sugar or keg and carbonate.

By following these professional steps for each beer style—Ale, Lager, Sour, and Stout—you can master the art of brewing at home and craft beers with rich and unique flavors!

Made in United States
Orlando, FL
30 July 2025